BARNEY OLDFIELD

The Life and Times
of America's Legendary Speed King

Other Books by William F. Nolan

OMNIBUS OF SPEED
(with Charles Beaumont)

ADVENTURE ON WHEELS
(with John Fitch)

BARNEY

OLDFIELD

THE LIFE AND TIMES OF

AMERICA'S LEGENDARY SPEED KING

By WILLIAM F. NOLAN

 G. P. PUTNAM'S SONS

NEW YORK

FOR RUSS CATLIN,
Honored Historian of Racing's Roaring Age.

AND FOR MY FATHER,
Who Lived it.

Contents

CONTENTS

INTRODUCTION

America, as a nation, has always been prone to hero worship. She romantically embraces the legendary and the mythical, and her idols must invariably be larger than life—demigods rather than men. When Davy Crockett died at the Alamo he passed into folklore; when Lindbergh flew the Atlantic he became an overnight legend; when Dwight D. Eisenhower swept into the presidency in 1952 Americans were electing an idol, a storied hero of the Second World War—and Ike's politics were, at best, a secondary consideration.

In the world of sports this national affinity for heroes and demigods takes firm root. Competitive sport offers a natural breeding ground and it is here, in the heat of battle on a baseball diamond, a football field, or a roped square of canvas, that America has created many of her greatest idols. Babe Ruth, the beloved "Sultan of Swat," was one of them. Notre Dame's immortal Knute Rockne was another. And who can ever forget the dynamite-fisted "Manassa Mauler," Jack Dempsey?

American automobile racing has also produced its heroes. In this colorful, danger-haunted sport, demanding nearly equal amounts of skill and courage, champions such as Wilbur Shaw, Rex Mays, Ted Horn and "Wild Bill" Vukovich live in our memories. Yet none of these epitomize auto racing in the legendary sense; they have not been elevated to the rarefied status of the demigod.

For Americans, only one name remains dominant in this century; only one man has passed into legend as a permanent symbol of speed and daring. Although he drove his last race some forty-three years ago, in 1918, his position is rock solid in our folklore. When the motor cop growls: "Say, who do you think you are, Barney Oldfield?" his meaning is as clear today as it was at the turn of the century.

Yet—what lies behind the name? What was Oldfield, as an individual, really like? Was he indeed the invincible champion, the unbeatable speed master? How did he manage to survive so many terrible crashes in his spectacular career? What of his personal loves, hopes, ambitions?

Four years ago, fired by a sudden desire to know more about the man himself (since my father, in his many recountings of those pioneer racing days, had supplied the legend), I asked the local library for a biography of Barney Oldfield. They informed me that such a book had never been written. Further investigation revealed that

10

while several excellent volumes were available tracing the development of the auto industry none contained a full history of Oldfield, and only a very few dealt in any comprehensive manner with his period of early-day racing. Therefore, with the need clearly established, I determined to write this book.

In *Barney Oldfield* I have not aimed at a specialized audience. In telling Barney's life story I have attempted to combine a man and an era—to recreate that dazzling and bedazzled, still wild and wonderful time of Teddy Roosevelt and his Rough Riders, of five-cent beer and derbies, of striped bathing suits and the Keystone Cops, Lillian Russell and the Florodora Sextette . . . of "Alexander's Ragtime Band," prohibition, Barrymore and Bernhardt—the time of the Gibson girl, of "Diamond Jim" Brady and the turkey trot. The Wright brothers were a part of it, and so were six-day bike races and Halley's comet. They sang sweet songs then: "Shine On, Harvest Moon," "In the Good Old Summertime," "Oh, You Beautiful Doll." Coiled brass tubas boomed on wooden bandstands at the county fair of a Sunday afternoon—and, for a nickel, you could watch Pearl White in *The Perils of Pauline*. This was the era of stern-eyed business giants: Pierpont Morgan, the Vanderbilts and the Astors; it was the era of McKinley, Taft and Wilson, of the Pan American Exposition and "Oh, you kid!"—of champagne in a slipper, the wasp waist, of cupid's bow lips and the Ziegfeld Follies. And, of course, it was the time of the horseless carriage—of the balky, spitting, cantankerous gasoline-powered automobile, a new, exclusively rich-man's toy in America—until one bold Ohio farmboy tamed it, and became immortal.

He was Barney Oldfield—rogue, rule-breaker, braggart, sentimentalist, gambler, showman, barroom brawler, dirt-track daredevil—a man without fear in a fabulous era.

This is his story.

WILLIAM F. NOLAN

HOLLYWOOD, CALIFORNIA

BARNEY OLDFIELD

*The Life and Times
of America's Legendary Speed King*

1

DUEL IN THE MICHIGAN DUST

The morning of October 25, 1902, dawned chill and gray over Michigan. The sky was a shifting mass of oppressive, slate-colored clouds, and by noon a gust of wind-driven rain had dampened the mile oval at Grosse Pointe, just east of Detroit. The popular horse track, proudly described by a local newspaper as "the most beautiful in the country," was originally laid out over a stretch of low-lying marshland bordering the Detroit River, and many spirited thoroughbreds had galloped to dusty victory on its dirt surface. However, on this particular afternoon, the five-mile main event (for the Manufacturers' Challenge Cup) was not to be contested by four-legged steeds. No, here at Grosse Pointe, before some 2,000 impatient spectators, that awesome turn-of-the-century phenomenon, the automobile, would unleash its frightening speed.

Excitement was in the air. The nation's automotive champion, Alexander Winton, millionaire founder of the Winton Motor Carriage Company in Cleveland, and the man responsible for America's first commercially successful motor car, was here to drive his fabled "Bullet," a machine capable of brutal track speeds in *excess* of 50 miles per hour. He was certain to vanquish the field, and with a well-dampened track a new record might be in the offing.

To understand properly the avid curiosity engendered by such an event, it must be borne in mind that America, in 1902, was still a land of the horse and buggy. Millions of Americans had never seen an automobile, and beyond the large cities the auto was all but unknown as a form of transportation. For example, auto registrations for the entire state of New York totaled just 909. Extensive four-wheeled travel was impossible, with only 178 miles of paved road throughout the country. Nevertheless, the auto had definitely progressed beyond the fad stage, and businessmen such as Winton knew that the quickest way to lure potential buyers was to prove a machine's durability and speed in open competition. Therefore, on this gray Saturday afternoon at Grosse Pointe, Alex Winton had his sights firmly set on another racing triumph for the Bullet.

(Scottish-born, Winton was nineteen when he landed in New York, in 1879, and at thirty had founded a bicycle company in Cleveland. By 1896 he put an automobile of his own design on the road, and was credited with the first commercial sale of an auto in the United States, two years later.)

Winton's main competitor in the five-miler was said to be the largest car in Detroit, the powerful Geneva Steamer. With its huge wheelbase, four massive boilers and tall stack, the Steamer dwarfed the low, flat-bodied Bullet, and trackside wagers were made that the Scotsman might well taste defeat at the hands of Bucknam, who was to pilot the big steam-driven vehicle. Only three other cars were entered: Shanks, in the Winton "Pup," White in his own White Steamer and the ex-cycling star Tom Cooper in an odd crimson-painted creation listed simply as "999."

Though it had not yet been tested under racing conditions, this unique automobile posed a solid threat to both Winton and Bucknam. Its monstrous four-cylinder engine promised to deliver almost twice the horsepower of the Bullet—75 against 40, and its rigid ashwood- and steel-plated chassis was stripped of all nonessential weight. However, handling the machine at speed was a serious problem, and brute strength was required to operate the heavy iron control bar. Due to the unyielding frame, any sizable chuck hole would pitch the entire car into the air, necessitating emergency action at the tiller. Also, since the stark machine lacked protective body-paneling, its driver was subjected to a continuous oil bath from the exposed crankshaft.

As the race was about to get under way, Winton, a dapper mustachioed man in spotless attire, climbed into the high seat of his Bullet with a confident smile. He waved a gloved hand to the crowd as a spectator

17

shouted: "We're betting on you, Alex. Make 'em eat your dust!"

Then Winton noticed that Tom Cooper was not in the bucket seat of 999. Instead, a husky youth with a shock of dark hair above his goggles sat nervously in Cooper's place.

"Who's that?" Winton inquired of an associate.

"Some kid named Oldfield. I hear this is his first race. Don't worry about him."

Winton nodded, more confident than ever. Since Cooper had been foolish enough to send a novice against veterans the potential threat of 999 could be disregarded.

Oldfield, trailing the other cars, seemed unsure of himself as the group rolled toward the starting tape, but as the flag snapped down he immediately shot ahead, sweeping around the first turn with a clear lead over a startled Winton. Although taken by surprise, the Scot fought back. After the first blistering mile his Bullet began to close the gap, steadily overhauling 999. The canny champion was proving his skill and speed, and it seemed that another important race would be added to Winton's victory string.

Glancing back at the onrushing Bullet, Oldfield set his jaw and opened the throttle. The red machine leaped forward with a deafening blast from its four exhausts. Sliding the turns in the same wide-open manner, dust pluming up behind him, Oldfield held the lead.

Winton was dropping back.

Skimming along, scant inches from the stout wooden fence encircling the track, the youth maintained full throttle, fighting the big car around the turns in a series of vicious slides.

By the third mile, with the Bullet's overstrained engine misfiring, Alex Winton was finished for the day.

The other competitors had never threatened—and as the contest neared its finish the highly touted Geneva Steamer was soundly beaten; Bucknam had been lapped by 999. By the end of the fifth mile, as he boomed under the flag, Barney came within a few feet of lapping the third-place runner, Shanks in the Pup.

An oil-grimed Oldfield had decisively won his first auto race. His time was 5:28—five minutes, 28 seconds—and he had covered the second mile in 1:04.8 for a new record.

Perched on the shoulders of the jubilant crowd, waving enthusiastically as photographers exploded flash powder in his face, Barney realized that he had tumbled Alexander Winton's speed crown into the Michigan dust. His life, from this day forward, would be filled with the unmuffled thunder of racing engines and the frenzied roar of crowds shouting for speed.

That victorious Saturday afternoon in late October of 1902 marked the beginning of a legend, a legend that would carry Oldfield's name to every town and city across the vast United States, a legend that would help to popularize the automobile in America years ahead of its time.

2

THE RAW YEARS

Barney Oldfield's father, Henry Clay Oldfield, was an Ohio farmer, whose father and grandfather before him had tilled the soil. A sun-bronzed, hard-muscled breed, they were outdoorsmen with a deep and instinctive love for the rich land which fed them. The family name derived from Aldfield—old field—in Yorkshire, and for several generations Oldfield's ancestors had lived as reed-thatch roofers in England.

When Henry Oldfield returned to Ohio after the Civil War, he bought a quarter section of farmland near the small village of Wauseon in the northwest part of the state, then proceeded to pay court to Sarah, the young daughter of Eli Yarnell, the town's blacksmith.

"Marry me, and I'll build you a fine log cabin," he promised her. "I've already got the land. Now I need a wife."

Sarah said yes. She had fallen deeply in love with Hank Oldfield, and now they would work the land and raise a family. To Sarah, strong like her new husband, hard work was one's normal lot in life, and until the children came she would share the daily burdens of a stern farm existence.

A baby girl, Bertha, was their firstborn, followed two years later by a son.

"During the war I made a promise to a bunkmate of mine, Berna Shoemaker," said Hank. "Told him if I ever had a son I'd name the boy after him. So that's what we'll do. We'll call him Berna."

Thus, on January 29, 1878, in a modest log cabin two miles north of Wauseon, York Township, Fulton County, Ohio, Berna Eli Oldfield was born. No baby in the state was more welcome.

America was a nation in flux during this era, when raw violence was coupled with scientific advancement. In 1879, while Billy the Kid was fighting in the Lincoln County Wars, Edison invented the incandescent bulb; in 1881, while the James Boys rode the outlaw trails in Missouri, New York City's complex elevated railway system was completed; in 1885, while Geronimo and his Apache warriors were cutting a bloody swath through Arizona and New Mexico, the invention of the linotype machine revolutionized the printing industry and opened the door to modern journalism.

As America grew, so did young Berna. He was soon attending elementary classes at the "little white school-house," at the corner of Elm and Clinton in Wauseon, while his parents struggled to eke out a bare living for Berna and his sister. In 1889, after a particularly severe winter, they came to a decision. They would leave the farm and head for Toledo. Henry was certain that he could find steady work there, and Sarah agreed. She knew that it would also mean better schooling for Berna, and she had long since lost her taste for the bitter, dawn-till-dark work on the farm.

Originally surrounded on three sides by vast swamps, Toledo had been developed by New Englanders who came down Lake Erie on their way to settle the West. Built on the banks of the Maumee River, the town was a center for the shipment of coal and iron ore. It was also a thriving rail center, with the great steam locomotives adding their strident bells and whistles to the deep bass moan of the lake freighters.

By 1892, the citizens of Toledo, along with the rest of America, had adopted cycling as a national pastime and the now familiar lyrics of "Daisy Bell" (". . . you'll look sweet upon the seat of a bicycle built for two") attested to the immense popularity of this challenger to the horse and buggy.

At fourteen, Berna Oldfield was also bitten by the cycling bug, and his primary aim in life was the acquisition of his own bicycle. He began saving pennies toward this goal. That summer, during his vacation from school, he talked himself into the job of water boy on a railroad section gang, earning a dollar a day for his efforts. On Sundays he'd spend most of the afternoon at the local fire house, hoping for a sudden conflagration. As "mascot," he was allowed to ride the big red hose wagon, while a snorting pair of powerful horses pulled it, at full gallop, through Toledo streets. Since he could not as yet afford a bicycle, the fire wagon had to suffice. Speed had already become a strong intoxicant to young Berna.

"Some day I'll own the fastest cycle in the whole wide world," he told his parents. "People will come from a thousand miles away, just to watch me ride it!"

Although, by 1893, a million bicycles were in use across the United States, another wheeled vehicle was eventually to displace them. This was the horseless carriage, the motor wagon, the road locomotive—or, as it soon came to be known, the automobile. No other invention would have such a profound and far-reaching effect on the nation's economy. Its history, up to this point, had been sporadic. As early as 1769 Captain Nicholas Cugnot had constructed a road-carriage in France, powered by steam, capable of almost three miles per hour, but it was not until 1876 that the first internal-combustion engine—of the type later to be universally adapted to gas-driven autos—was invented, by N. A. Otto, of Germany. Nine years later, utilizing an engine designed by Gottlieb Daimler, Karl Benz was credited with producing the first successful gasoline-powered motor vehicle, a weird, tri-wheeled affair which was road-tested in Mannheim, Germany, in 1885. Daimler then took his engine to France, and M. Levassor (of Panhard and Levassor) used it to power the world's first gas-driven horseless carriage.

Therefore, by 1893, although the average citizen of the United States was blissfully unaware of its existence, the horseless carriage was an overseas reality. Its full potential, however, rested with America, and in various sections of the country a handful of farsighted men were working independently on primitive machines of their own design. They included Charles and Frank Duryea, Elwood Haynes, Ransom E. Olds and Henry Ford. On September 22, in Springfield, Massachusetts, Frank Duryea tested what was later recognized as America's first automobile, a crudely fashioned vehicle which was little more than a buggy with an engine awkwardly attached to its underside.

This test in Springfield marked the dawn of the motoring age.

During the fall of 1893, Berna Oldfield (still dreaming of bicycles) permanently laid aside his school books to take a full-time job with his father at a Toledo mental institution. The money Berna brought home hawking the Toledo *Blade* and *Bee* had not been sufficient to meet family needs, and so he joined Henry Oldfield as a kitchen helper at the asylum. The work was arduous and ill-paying, and Berna was in a continual state of unease around the patients. Therefore, when he was offered the chance to become a bellhop at Toledo's renowned hostelry, the Boody House, he readily accepted. With his quick smile and gregarious nature Oldfield was a popular member of the staff, garnering enough in tips to convince him that a winning personality paid off. Here, at the Boody, he began to develop his natural ability to deal with the public. It was here, also, that his famous nickname was born.

"Hey, Barney!" shouted the bell captain, of a busy afternoon. "The gent in 211 needs some ice water."

"The name's Berna," Oldfield corrected him.

"Nuts to Berna," snapped the older boy. "That's for sissies. You're no sissy, are ya?"

Oldfield reddened, fists doubling. He considered the question. Then he sighed. "Okay," he told the bell captain, "around here I'm Barney."

The nickname stuck. Even his family began using it—and when he again switched jobs, to become an elevator operator at the Monticello Hotel, the salary checks were made out to Barney Oldfield.

Bicycle racing had now become a universal sport, and the exploits of daring speed-cyclists provided exciting news copy. Young Barney religiously perused each lurid account, envisioning himself at the head of a frustrated pack of desperately pedaling champions, none of whom could catch him. His dreams began to assume a more solid shape when he was at last able to purchase a cycle of his own, a standard Dauntless with pneumatic tires. But the heavy Dauntless failed to give him the speed he required and he knew it would prove hopeless in competition.

Then Oldfield made a discovery. One of the Monticello's tenants, R. D. Merrill, owned a lightweight Cleveland cycle which he stored each night in the hotel basement. It was a simple matter for Barney to appropriate the bike each evening after Mr. Merrill had retired, returning it to its berth before the owner awakened. Thus, in numerous moonlit excursions over the deserted streets of Toledo, Barney practiced fast riding.

In the spring of the following year, at sixteen, Berna Eli Oldfield entered his first race.

3

WITH THE WILD TWO-WHEELERS

Seventeen youthful cyclists lined up in east Toledo on May 30, 1894, for the demanding cross-country event which was routed through Perrysburg and Maumee, ending in Walbridge Park. The starting field included some of the town's best amateur riders, and scant attention was given to the entry of B. Oldfield, on a borrowed Royal Flush model. In such a rugged contest, covering some 18 miles of varied terrain, a beginner was not expected to finish among the first ten.

Barney had other ideas. In his mind's eye, the victory was already his, and he was coolly determined to demonstrate his basic superiority.

Once the race got under way, however, Oldfield's coolness vanished with the rush of passing cycles. He was already lagging sadly back, despite his best efforts. But the boy learned fast. He noted that the leaders hunched very low over the handle bars; he'd been sitting too erect.

He began to move up, and when the field swept through Perrysburg like a formation of low-flying geese he was closing rapidly on the leaders.

Pedaling furiously, breath burning like hot smoke in his lungs, Barney passed one competitor after another. As the cyclists dipped into Walbridge Park, Oldfield was riding a tight third, and in the finishing stretch, with a final burst of effort from his aching leg muscles, he sailed over the line to score a hard-won second place.

That evening, still tasting the near victory, he flourished his prize before the amused eyes of his parents.

"Look, Ma, I won a gen-u-ine guaranteed diamond ring!" He twisted the stone until it sparkled under the lamplight. "And do you know what the man told me it was worth?"

"I have no idea," smiled Sarah Oldfield.

"Said it was worth a *fortune!* No foolin' he did. Said it was worth twenty-five dollars!"

His self-confidence restored by this initial performance in competition, Barney grew more ambitious. He financed a trip to Detroit (with money he received by pawning the diamond ring) and boldy entered the Hilsendegen Bicycle Race, a punishing 25-miler on Belle Island. Outclassed and exhausted, he dropped from the contest a few miles short of the finish, complaining of a severe pain in his chest. Here, as in Toledo, he had learned something important: victory called for more than skill and a fighting spirit; it involved a high degree of physical stamina, coupled with an ability to "pace" over the entire distance, to gauge one's strength, apportioning it out gradually and reserving just enough for the final sprint to the wire.

Other races followed, and Barney also discovered that serious competition among some of the cycle veterans often became a case of dangerous wheel-tangling, handlebar-hooking tactics employed to eliminate stubborn novices.

When Oldfield returned to his elevator job at the Monticello that winter his collarbone had been broken twice in vicious spills.

Anxious for personal independence, Barney's parents had invested what they'd been able to put aside in a small ice-cream parlor on Main Street in Toledo. Alarmed by their son's intense participation in what Hank considered "a fool's game," they asked Barney to join them in the new venture.

"You're going to end up with every bone in your body broken at this rate," his father said. "You've got to settle down and make us proud of you."

"That's just what I figure to do," declared Barney. "Only—you've gotta let me do it *my* way. I've been contacted by the Dauntless factory. They want me to ride for them at Canton in the state championship meet." Barney hesitated. "And I said I would."

Hank Oldfield drew a long breath. He turned to his wife. "He's almost a man, Sarah. And a man makes his own decisions." He grinned at Barney. "Go to Canton, son. And good luck!"

The Ohio State Championship Races, run in the spring

of 1895, proved to be a turning point in Barney Oldfield's life. He did well enough (finishing second in three events and winning a pair of silver medals and a gold watch) to attract the eye of a local representative for the Stearns Bicycle Company, and was subsequently hired as a parts salesman. He also met a girl in Canton, Beatrice Loretta Oatis, just under twenty, and Irish to the blue of her eyes. Barney called her Bridget, enchanted by her soft, shy smile, by the graceful way she moved, by the big-city clothes she wore. The spell was complete. Within a week he had asked her to marry him.

"Not until you're sure you want me," she replied firmly. "And not until *I'm* sure. Let's wait a year, then I'll come to Toledo and we'll see how we both feel about one another."

Dizzy with love, Barney returned home. He'd been unable to change Bridget's mind and he only hoped she'd keep her promise.

Oldfield soon discovered that selling bicycle parts was a haphazard occupation at best; a man could starve in an off week when the commissions were not coming in. If he expected to marry Bridget he'd have to make a substantial amount of money in order to impress her with his financial stability. It was obvious he could not remain a salesman.

Certainly there was money to be made in the boxing profession. John L. Sullivan, "The Boston Strong Boy," had demonstrated this; so had "Gentleman Jim" Corbett. Victory in the prize ring meant big money, and Barney saw no reason why he could not become an overnight success as a boxer. This bland assumption stemmed from his natural abiding confidence in his own ability, and from the opinion of local pug Dan Bailiff, who had offered assistance in coaching Oldfield. After one look at Barney's six-foot, 190-pound physique, Bailiff pronounced it "the body of a gladiator." Barney was delighted.

"I'm going up to Lima to get in shape," Dan said. "Come with me, kid, and I'll teach you all I know. We'll call you 'The Toledo Terror'! How does that sound?"

"Great!" Barney threw a roundhouse right at an invisible opponent. "Boy, just watch me wade in!"

The Toledo Terror never reached the ring.

In Lima, Ohio, Oldfield contracted typhoid fever and was rushed to a hospital bed. (As he later admitted: "I got over the boxing fever about the time I got over typhoid.")

On Thanksgiving Day, while Barney was recuperating, America's first automobile race was run in Chicago. This historic date was November 28, 1895—and the star of the affair was Frank Duryea in a slightly revamped version of the machine he'd tested in Springfield just two years before. Its one-cyclinder, water-cooled gasoline engine only produced four horsepower, but according to *Autocar*, the Duryea was capable of "magnificent time... a rate of eight miles per hour." The 52.4-mile event (from Jackson Park to Evanston and back) was sponsored by Chicago's *Times-Herald*, and the $2,000 first prize attracted an "international" field. Entries were received for 11 vehicles, but only six of these actually reached the starting line. The weather was severe, with a foot of mushy snow on the roads, putting three of the competitors (the Sturges Electric, the Morris Salom Electrobat and the La Vergne) immediately out of contention. A Benz-powered Roger, driven by R. H. Macy, might have won but for a series of misfortunes which included running into a horse cart, a sleigh, and a taxi. After a fourth collision with a carriage Macy called it quits. H. Mueller, in another Benz, was picking up on the leading Duryea when he lost consciousness from the bitter cold and buried his machine in a snowdrift. The relief driver eventually finished the race, over an hour and a half behind the Duryea. It had taken the winner some 10 hours to cover the full 52.4 miles, but two of these were consumed by roadside repairs. Duryea's overall average for the run: 5.1 mph.

The importance of that initial Chicago race cannot be overemphasized. Historian Rudolph Anderson pointed out: "All of the different types of motorized exhibitions were to grow out of this event—road races, speedway bowls, high-speed demonstrations, endurance tests, reliability runs, hill climbs, transcontinental tours, automobile shows and the mammoth displays at the World Fairs." The great showman, P. T. Barnum, was so impressed with the Duryea's showing that he arranged to have the amazing machine sent on tour with his circus, where it shared top billing with the trapeze acts and the elephants.

For the Duryea Brothers, the victory in Chicago encouraged them to become auto manufacturers—and the Duryea Motor Wagon Company produced 10 cars within the following year. America's position in the auto world was now solidly established.

The country's automotive progress had little immediate effect upon Barney Oldfield. He was naturally somewhat interested in the new contraptions, but doubted that they were much more than a passing fad. When the Stearns factory invited him to ride one of their Yellow Flyers (at $75 per month and expenses) he was certain that his future lay with the fleet two-wheelers. In 1896 he signed a contract with E. C. Stearns to compete on the team—but the League of American Wheelmen threatened him with blacklisting unless he turned professional. They would have nothing to do with "paid amateurs."

Billing himself "The Bicycle Champion of Ohio" (because he won second place in the state competition for Class A at Dayton that season on a Stearns), Barney hired a manager, Ed Tellum, and with rider Fred Titus formed the Racycle Racing Team.

"We circulated through the South and Midwest," Oldfield later remarked. "If Fred didn't win, I usually did. But it was rough. We pawned a whole bushel of medals, rings and trophies in order to pay our hotel bills."

In August of '96 Beatrice Oatis kept her promise; she met Barney in Toledo and they were married in that city on the twenty-fifth of the month. Oldfield was not ready for marriage, and his affection for his new bride was little more than a youthful "crush." The relationship was destined to be an unhappy one.

For the moment, however, Barney and Beatrice were content to be a vital part of the rollicking Gay Nineties, and their attitude toward life seemed to be perfectly summed up by two lines of popular verse, widely quoted in that era:

> Laugh and the world laughs with you;
> Weep and you weep alone.

This was the time of mutton-leg sleeves and detachable cuffs, of saloon-smashing Carrie Nation, Buffalo Bill Cody and his Wild West Show, of Mark Twain, of Lillian Russell, of peacock feathers and marble-topped tables... a time of the "hootchy-cootchy," of gold-trimmed mustache cups and wooden Indians.

Bicycle racing was in vogue; contests between the wild two-wheelers lured record crowds, and star riders were very much in demand.

Oldfield was maturing as a top competitor, but his aggressive style made him rather unpopular among several fellow riders. A variety of cycles were used in competition—from two-man tandems to seven-man septuplets —and whenever Barney became wheelman his intense desire to win often resulted in spectacular upsets. On the board saucers this meant that many a sharp wood splinter had to be painfully removed from Oldfield's hide.

During these years, when the Klondike Gold Rush and the Spanish-American War occupied headlines, Oldfield barnstormed the Midwest, supplementing his seasonal income with factory work and the sale of cycle parts. In 1898, about the time Teddy Roosevelt was charging up San Juan Hill at the head of his Rough Riders, records show that Barney was competing on a four-man quadruplet at Indianapolis. (Recalled Oldfield: "We got a fourth in the race, but since three others guys were ahead of me on the same bike it's hard to say *where* I finished!")

During the spring of 1899 he was approached by a promoter who wanted a "star" name to publicize an upcoming race from Blair, Nebraska, to Omaha.

"I'm your little huckleberry," grinned Oldfield. "You bill me as 'The Bicycle Champion of Ohio,' and we're in business."

"One other thing," said the promoter. "Here in Nebraska each of our boys has a special formula for winning. You know, some of them chew salt, or wear a bag of onions at their belt, or munch on carrots. What we need is a real keen formula for you."

"Lemme think," said Barney, "and I'll come up with one."

On the evening before the race Oldfield purchased a bottle of bourbon at a local saloon. "Steam off the label," he told the bartender, flashing a silver dollar.

The next morning Barney appeared on the starting line with the bottle tied around his neck. He was approached by curious spectators and asked what the bottle contained.

"Vinegar," confided the champ. "Couldn't win without it."

Actually, Oldfield *did* win this race, but the achievement had nothing to do with vinegar (or bourbon). As Barney trailed the leaders over the last miles into Omaha the clouds opened up, reducing the dirt roads to gumbo. Oldfield cannily hoisted his National Chainless to the railroad tracks and bumped to victory over the solid roadbed.

The occasion was saluted with proper headlines: "Ohio Champion, Trained on Vinegar, Wins 25-Mile Classic." (And Barney later swore that when next he passed through Omaha all the aspirant local cyclists, to a man, carried bottles of vinegar around their necks.)

As Oldfield matured as a competitor the automobile also matured as a form of transportation, gaining a wider degree of acceptance with each passing month.

In November of 1896 Thomas Edison had stated: "Ten years from now you will be able to buy a horseless vehicle for what you have to pay today for a wagon and a pair of horses." A year later, Cholly Knickerbocker, society's favorite columnist, took his first ride in a self-powered carriage and shared his awe with readers of the New York *Journal:* "There is a sense of incompleteness about it. As I returned the wicked glances of the bicycle ladies on the boulevard . . . I seemed to be sitting on the edge of a huge pushcart propelled by an invisible force and guided by a hidden hand."

In 1899 the War Department cautiously added three

automobiles to its inventory with the following statement: "These motor vehicles have been purchased for
the use of officers. Each is equipped so that a mule may
be hitched to it should it refuse to run."

By the year's close, McKinley had become the first
President to ride in a horseless carriage (having taken a
short jaunt in a Stanley Steamer), and Alexander Winton
had made his record-breaking long-distance auto trip
(707.4 miles) from Cleveland to New York, in his own
eight-horsepower machine, averaging 15 miles per hour.

Over the space of three years, auto registrations had
rocketed from 16 in 1896 to 3,200 in 1899, and though
America still rang to the blacksmith's hammer, the sput-
ter of a gasoline engine was beginning to be heard across
the land.

In 1900 the first big auto show was held at Madison
Square Garden, with no less than 31 machines on display.
Even Andrew Carnegie and J. Pierpont Morgan had
joined the autoists, lending their vast prestige to the
budding industry.

Of far more direct concern to Barney Oldfield was the
fact that one of his cycling pals, Tom Cooper, had won
the coveted Bicycle Championship of America during
the 1899 season, and was using some of the prize money
to purchase a gas-powered motor-tandem in England.
(This cycle had reputedly traveled at a 40-mph speed
around London's Crystal Palace bowl.)

"I'm bringing the tandem back to the States with me,"
he wrote Oldfield early in 1900, "and the two of us ought
to be able to set a few records with it."

Inspired by the news, Barney outdid himself that August in Omaha. Although he lost two straight match heats against Iver "The Terrible Swede" Lawson, he came very close to breaking the world's mile record in a fierce run over the Midway track. A local news clipping verifies his feat: "Oldfield rode like a demon, fairly electrifying the spectators as he shot meteorlike around the track. He finished the mile in a fraction less than two minutes, which is within two-fifths of a second of the world's record presently held by Lawson."

By mid-October, Tom was back from Europe and Barney enthusiastically tried out the motorcycle. "She sure goes! When do we give her a run?"

"We'll take her down to Grosse Pointe this month," said Cooper.

They took the imported motor-tandem to the Detroit horse track in order to stage an exhibition run around the dirt oval, but their performance was completely overshadowed by an unknown mechanic-inventor named Henry Ford, who managed to defeat Alex Winton that afternoon with a twenty-six-horsepower racing machine of his own design.*

"These damn fancy automobiles are nothin' but a fad," Barney growled to Cooper, as they wheeled away the tandem. "When are the stupid people gonna wake up and quit yellin' like banshees every time they see one?"

"Maybe you're the one who'll be waking up," declared Cooper. "The auto is no fad, Barney. To tell you the truth,

* This win preceded Oldfield's 999 Grosse Pointe victory over Winton (as related in the first chapter) by exactly two years.

I got plenty excited myself out there today, watching that Ford go. I'm quitting the cycle game anyhow. Maybe I'll buy me a real fast machine and win a few auto races for a change. Looks like fun."

Barney snorted. "I wouldn't be seen dead in one of the damn things."

In 1900, at the century's turn, the United States, from the Alleghenies to the Pacific Coast, was still largely a frontier nation. Even the ever-expanding railroads had not as yet penetrated many parts of the rugged western plains, where travel by stagecoach still prevailed. Therefore, Oldfield's failure to appreciate the potential of the automobile was understandable. (Even the "mirror of public taste," the Sears, Roebuck catalogue of 1900, failed to devote even a single page to autos or automotive accessories.)

Tom Cooper, however, was auto-minded, and he kept his word about his future plans; he announced his retirement from cycling. But he did not immediately move into auto racing. In the late fall of 1901 he bought a coal mine in Colorado.

"Come west with me this winter and we'll both get rich," he told Barney. "I'll make you a full partner, and you can pay me out of the profits."

Oldfield, fascinated by the sudden possibility of becoming an influential mine owner, agreed to accompany Tom to Colorado and work through the winter there with him. He and Beatrice had separated, and it was as good a time as any to plunge into a new business.

4

A MILE A MINUTE!

The Cow Creek Coal Mine, located near Montrose and Ouray, in Colorado's San Juan Mountains, proved a doomed venture from the outset.

By winter's end, after months of backbreaking labor, Cooper and Oldfield had netted approximately $1,000 between them, but Tom insisted that Barney take his full half share.

"Hell, you don't owe me a cent," Barney protested. "I promised to pay you for taking me in as a partner didn't I?"

"You ought to kick me instead," Tom grinned. "No, I'll stand my loss. You deserve your five hundred. I've still got plenty in Detroit put away safe in the bank. I'm going back there and look up Henry Ford, maybe have him build a racer for me."

"Then I'd like to take the motor-tandem out to Salt

Lake City," said Barney. "I could really make it go on that Salt Palace bowl."

"Sure," Cooper told him. "Only don't call me in to dig the splinters out of your rump. From here on, I'm *strictly* an automobilist."

America, in 1902, was sharply divided into those who were for the horse and those who were for the auto. There was no middle ground. (Of course, this difference of opinion involved only the citizens of the larger cities, since automobiles were still virtually unheard of in the hinterlands.) When a road locomotive would come chugging explosively down a busy street, startled horses would neigh in fear, pawing the sky and often upsetting carts and wagons. Fruits and vegetables would be dumped while red-faced grocers shook their fists at the passing autoist. A cartoon in *Life* portrayed an irate horse-and-buggy owner standing by his wrecked vehicle as a fast auto disappeared around a bend. He had a shotgun at his shoulder, aimed at the fleeing car. The caption read: "Must we take the law into our own hands?"

Much of the bitterness was directed against the noisy, backfiring gasoline engines, and it was generally believed that this nuisance would soon be done away with. Of the 909 autos registered in New York State that year 485 were steam-powered, and it seemed quite logical that the quiet, smooth, economical steam engine would displace the greasy, troublesome, complicated gasoline engine. (The Stanley Steamer boasted of utilizing only 13 moving parts in its two-cylinder power plant—and no transmission or gearshift was needed.) The battery-driven Electrics were still to be seen, but they were impractical over any extended distance, and were not seriously considered by those looking toward America's automotive future. Steam, therefore, seemed to provide the ideal source of power.

Many authorities are firmly convinced that all cars would be steam-driven today were it not for a dark rumor that was widespread at the century's turn. "Look out for them devilish boilers," one neighbor would warn another. "They'll explode and blow your family to kingdom come!" The fact that even the earliest Steamers were protected by safety devices to keep the boiler pressure from rising too high did not have any effect on the rumormongers. Gradually, spreading public fear put the Steamers out of business, and after 1902 sales declined steadily to the vanishing point.

While Tom Cooper headed for Detroit and a meeting with Henry Ford, Oldfield took the motor-tandem and a standard Tribune "Blue Streak" pedal bike to the big board track in Salt Lake City. There he banked the remainder of his $500, rented a room near the Salt Palace (for $3 a week) and prepared to set some records.

He began by overhauling the cycle's engine, raising the compression after removing the cylinder head and filing down the top of the cylinder. Noting that he was able to extract more speed from the unit by day than by night (Utah races were run under lights), he piped the hot exhaust around the carburetor, which produced excellent results. (As Barney later said of the tandem: "She went like blazes!")

Oldfield rode the revamped machine to a new mile mark, then (having transferred the engine to his Tribune single-seater) won a 10-mile motorcycle race on the high-banked board saucer in the record time of 13 minutes, 10 seconds, covering the fastest mile in 1:21. It seemed that Barney was on the verge of a new career in motorcycling when a letter arrived from Detroit which dramatically altered his life.

It came from Tom Cooper, and in it the ex-champion told Barney that he had formed a partnership with Ford to build a pair of special high-speed racing cars, and that the project was already well under way. They needed another mechanic and Cooper urged Barney to join the small group, hinting strongly that he might get a chance to drive one of the racers.

Granting the possibility that he could have been mistaken about the future of automotive competition, Oldfield decided to accept Cooper's offer. This new sport might eventually provide a far greater source of income than cycling—and he found himself excited at the possibility of handling a big four-wheeled racing car. Withdrawing his money from the Wells Fargo bank, he bought a one-way ticket to Detroit.

When Cooper joined Ford it was agreed that Tom would shoulder most of the financial burden, and that the plans, primary design and materials would be Ford's responsibility. With a draftsman, C. Harold Wills, and a chief mechanic, Ed "Spider" Huff, they rented a shop at 81 Park Place and set to work on the racing cars. As the two machines took shape more help was needed, and Cooper had written Oldfield after suggesting him to Ford as "a man who lived for speed."

When Barney arrived at the Detroit workshop, in late September of 1902, the cars were in their final stages, but to the cyclist they seemed little more than "bedframes on wheels."

Cooper explained their starkness. "Every pound of excess weight will slow us down," he said, "so we've mounted the engines on stripped chassis. Everything is functional. We didn't build these for looks."

"You sure as hell didn't," nodded Oldfield, circling the two vehicles. "They're ugly as sin! You sure they'll even run?"

"We tested one of them at Grosse Pointe," Ford put in. "We've still got some problems to overcome, but both cars should be ready for another run this weekend."

The basic specifications on these machines were explained to Oldfield. Each engine was equipped with special cast-iron cylinder walls, allowing a seven-inch bore and a seven-inch stroke, which meant that they were the largest four-cylinder power plants used in any car of the period, producing a theoretical maximum of 80 horsepower. Piston displacement was 1,080 cubic inches (or approximately *four* times that of a present-day V-8 unit). Each cylinder had its own exhaust pipe which spurted blue flame as the engine roared at 700 revolutions per minute. Lacking transmissions, the tiller-steered cars had but one forward speed. A single bucket seat was mounted on the frame behind the engine, and the exposed radiator loomed in front like an upturned coffin.

Accounts vary as to precisely how these machines became the exclusive property of Tom Cooper, but a letter from Ford's wife, Clara, verifies the sale and sets the date of purchase as October 13 (just 12 days before Oldfield's triumph over Winton at Grosse Pointe). Ford's temporary disenchantment with the cars apparently stemmed from their second test at the dirt oval.

That weekend, as Ford had promised, the two racers (one painted a bright red, the other a crisp lemon yellow) were towed out to the Grosse Pointe track.

"Oil 'em up, Barney," instructed Cooper.

Oldfield squirted the open crankshaft, filled the sight-feed oilers, then inserted a long crank handle and attempted to start the engine of the yellow car. No response. Finally, his shirt sweat-soaked to his back, he gave up and turned to the red machine. He cranked vigorously; the engine sputtered to life, gasped, then died. Further cranking did not remedy the situation. The cars were totally inoperative.

Ford was plainly discouraged, and back at the shop he voiced this discouragement. "I'm sorry, gentlemen, but I don't think we can continue." (He'd been negotiating with a wealthy businessman, Alex Malcomson, for the establishment of his own motor company to produce non-racing automobiles, and now felt that he could not endanger this venture with a disaster in competition.)

"You mean you want to *quit,* give up the whole project?" demanded Cooper.

"I don't see how I can allow my name to be connected with a probable failure. These machines are obviously not going to win any races."

Further conversation ensued, during which the figure of $800 was mentioned for Henry's share in both cars. The sale was transacted, with full ownership reverting to Cooper.

With Ford's unofficial blessing, Tom and Barney, aided by Spider Huff, immediately set to work in an effort to make the two machines operable. When an invitation arrived from Carl Fisher (later to gain fame as a founding father of the Indianapolis Speedway) asking them if they could bring the racers to a meet in Dayton, Ohio, Oldfield urged Cooper to accept.

"Okay. Wire Fisher. Tell him we'll be there," said Cooper. "With some luck, we'll be able to show Henry just how wrong he was in selling out."

But at Dayton, on October 18, luck seemed to be the afternoon's missing ingredient. The yellow machine still refused to start.

"If the other one doesn't fire up, we're done," Tom admitted. "Maybe Ford was right after all."

Then the red machine came to life with an explosive roar, bringing a wide smile to the face of promoter Carl Fisher. "Now, *there,*" he shouted above the din, "is a motor car!"

At this moment the engine abruptly ceased firing.

Huff, Oldfield and Cooper exchanged despairing glances. Then Barney broke the miserable silence. "I don't think the gasoline is getting to the mixer quick enough. But maybe I can fix it."

Barney quickly cut a hole in the gas tank and inserted a length of rubber hose, taping it in. With the engine sputtering again—yet threatening to quit any second— Huff climbed behind the tiller and Cooper scrambled up beside him. Barney leaped aboard behind the driving seat and began to use his cyclist's lung power on the hose. Immediately the engine smoothed—and the red car was under way at last for its first exhibition run amid wild cheers from the assembled onlookers. (Oldfield later referred to himself as "a human gasoline pump" on this, his first dusty ride in a racing automobile.)

"Better slow down, Spider, or we'll go right through the damned fence!" yelled Cooper as they skidded a turn.

"Yeah," Huff yelled back, "she sure goes like '999.'"

His reference to the New York Central's record-breaking steam locomotive impressed Cooper.

"Then that's what we'll call her," Tom declared, as the car rolled to a stop. "From now on, she's '999.'"

The yellow car was put aside for the moment, and all work was concentrated on 999. Alexander Winton would be at Grosse Pointe in just a week to send his Bullet against all comers, and Cooper wanted to take him on. With the help of a local coppersmith, they redesigned the engine's "mixing pot" (ancestor to the modern car-

buretor) in a vacant storeroom in Toledo, finishing just
in time to ship 999 back to Detroit by boat.

Unloading the car at wharfside, Barney approached
his old friend "Hot Dog" John, who ran a lunchwagon
in town, and asked him for the loan of his horse.

"If we try to fire up this rig here," he explained, "we'll
give every nag in Detroit heart failure. Sound's loud
enough to half kill a man."

The lunchman said he understood, and turned his
animal over to Barney.

"We'll tow her out to East Jefferson Avenue," said
Barney, "then crank up and drive onto the track. What'll
we do with your horse?"

"Just turn him loose," said John. "He knows the way
back."

They reached Grosse Pointe in time for a full day's
practice. Cooper and Huff each took the racer around
the choppy oval, complaining to Barney of steering diffi-
culties.

"She's a bear to handle," said Cooper. "Wide open,
she'd be death on wheels."

"Lemme have a crack at the tiller," pleaded Barney.
"I'm sure I could keep her in line."

"This is no bicycle," Cooper warned. "You could break
your neck out there."

"It's my neck," asserted Oldfield. "How about it, Tom?
I didn't come all the way from Salt Lake City to squirt
an oil can."

"Like you say, it's *your* neck."

Within minutes Oldfield was circling the mile oval

faster than Huff or Cooper, registering an impressive lap of 1:06. The choice was obvious; Barney would drive 999 against the Bullet.

"Well," grinned Oldfield, "this damn chariot may kill me, but they will say afterward that I was goin' like hell when she took me over the bank!"

The following day, on the cold, clouded afternoon of October 25, 1902, the bicycle rider from Ohio defeated America's automotive champion, Alexander Winton. And certainly the reporter for the Detroit *News* who had written his impressions of Oldfield in that epic race ("Hatless, his long, tawny hair flying out behind him with the speed of his mount, seeming a dozen times on the verge of capsize . . .") would be the last to deny that Barney had indeed been "goin' like hell."

Henry Ford had also been an enthusiastic spectator at Grosse Pointe, and after warmly congratulating Oldfield and Cooper he headed for the local newspaper offices, anxious to receive proper credit as 999's designer. As a result of this publicity, with the financial backing of Alex Y. Malcomson, the Ford Motor Company was launched in November, and the designer-builder at the age of thirty-nine began his long climb toward vast fame and incalculable riches.

Oldfield, too, had gained instant acclaim; the win in 999 had netted him more popularity than all of his cycling victories combined, and he announced to the press that he would attempt to become the first American to break officially the magic mile-a-minute mark on a dirt track. Tom Cooper would sponsor the attempt.

The Cooper-Oldfield invasion of big-time auto racing was news. The sport had hitherto been the exclusive property of those wealthy enough to indulge their interest in it; men such as Winton, William K. Vanderbilt, John Jacob Astor, W. Gould Brokaw, Frank LaRoche and Foxhall Keene. However, Oldfield was only the first of many ex-cyclists who would turn this "gentleman's sport" into a rough-and-tumble moneymaking profession. The stage was set: the immense success of horse racing during the 1800s provided scores of mile and half-mile dirt tracks, complete with permanent grandstands. Almost every town had its fairground oval—with thousands of customers eager and willing to pay for the privilege of seeing a thunderous racing automobile in action.

However, not everyone was delighted with 999. One British journalist, upon witnessing a noisy demonstration run, commented: "This machine is the materialization of a nightmare, which has so grossly distorted the popular idea of the motor car that it should be disowned by all true automobilists."

Although he made several subsequent runs with 999 that year, Oldfield was unable to crack officially the elusive mile-a-minute mark. When he returned to Toledo for the winter he was determined to get the job done in 1903.

As the season opened in April, Oldfield suggested they

engage a manager to handle racing commitments, and Glenn Stuart, "the Kalamazoo celery king," was hired in this capacity. Since 999's balky sister machine was now in operative condition, Stuart had the yellow paint covered with crimson and the name changed from "The Arrow" to "The Red Devil." Cooper was signed to drive it at Indianapolis that June against Oldfield in 999.

Prior to this meet, Stuart arranged to have Barney ship 999 to the Empire City track in Yonkers, New York, for a run against Charles Ridgeway's fast Peerless. Oldfield was to receive twenty-five per cent of the gate receipts for his appearance.

The well-publicized match race was held on Memorial Day, May 30, and attracted a cheering crowd of 6,000. Oldfield won two straight heats over the Peerless (making the third unnecessary), and collected $1,300 for the afternoon. His share in the split with Cooper and Stuart amounted to $650—a truly fabulous sum when measured against the $2 a day he had received as a factory hand the previous winter. He immediately caught a train for Ohio.

"Look, Dad!" he shouted when his father met him at the station. "I made all this in *one* day!" He waved the money above his head. "And you know who gets it, every *penny* of it?"

Henry Oldfield was confused. "No—no, I don't."

"It goes to pay off the mortgage," smiled Barney. "You and Mom won't have to worry any more about losing the house. Now it's yours."

The older man could not reply. With tears in his eyes, he embraced his son.

"And there's gonna be plenty more where this came from," declared Barney. "I'm heading for Indianapolis next week—and this time I'm going to hit a mile a minute if I have to *fly* around the track!"

The starting field at the Indianapolis Fairgrounds (six years before the opening of the famed Speedway in that city) included several top drivers and cars, but 999 was the center of attention as Barney wheeled it onto the mile dirt oval for a warm-up run.

Carl Fisher, co-promoter of the meet, posed for a publicity shot next to the car, then told Barney: "There'll be an extra $250 in cash for you if you circle this track in under sixty seconds. Think you can do it, boy?"

Oldfield snorted. "Just hang that bag of lettuce on the fence past the finish line and kiss it goodbye. You'll have your record."

In the second heat of the day, after passing Cooper's Red Devil, Barney waved to Fisher in the judge's stand. He was "going for broke." The crimson car slashed around the first turn in a pillar of dust, then with Oldfield maintaining full throttle, took the second in the same hair-raising fashion. At the end of the mile he rolled 999 to a smoking stop.

"Did I make it, Carl?"

"You sure did," Fisher told him. "You broke sixty seconds wide open!"

On June 20, 1903, with a clocked time of fifty-nine and three-fifths seconds, Barney Oldfield had become the first man in the nation to drive a gas-powered auto officially at the "incredible" speed of a mile a minute.

5

DEATH BY BULLET

After his record-breaking dash at Indianapolis, newspapers across the United States were hailing Oldfield as "America's Premier Driver," and he was asked to give his impressions of just what it was like to travel at such a harrowing pace.

Under the headline "Going A Mile A Minute!" Barney was quoted in lurid detail: "You have every sensation of being hurled through space. The machine is throbbing under you with its cylinders beating a drummer's tattoo, and the air tears past you in a gale. In its maddening dash through the swirling dust the machine takes on the attributes of a sentient thing . . . I tell you, gentlemen: no man can drive faster and live!"

Oldfield's press agent elaborated on the dangers inherent in mile-a-minute speed: "Wind resistance is something awful. The chest of a driver is forced in, and his
54

pumping plant must be marvelously strong to resist the tremendous pressure in order to inhale sufficient air for the performance of its functions. Average lungs can't overcome the outward force and the result is like strangulation. Blood rushes to the head, temporary but complete paralysis of mind over body occurs and instantly the driver loses consciousness and control."

Yet, despite these dramatic declarations, Barney smashed his own record late the following month at the Empire City track with 999 in what was to be his final race in the famous car. *The Automobile* vividly summed up this run: ". . . Then Oldfield, with a roar like unto a passing comet, skidded around the far turn and flashed past the howling, horn-tooting crowd . . . He swung the iron steering bar hard to the left and the rear wheels slid sideways for a distance of 50 feet, throwing up a huge cloud of dirt that drove the spectators back from the fence . . . in an exhibition that caused the whole great crowd to gulp and gasp. Men were white-faced and breathless, while women covered their eyes and sank back, overcome by the utter recklessness of it all. When the judges hung out 55⅘ seconds as the time the riot of sound broke loose afresh."

Now fully aware of the money-making potential of auto racing, Barney decided to leave 999 with Cooper and go to work for Alexander Winton driving the Scot's fast, new Bullet No. 2. The contract which Winton offered was too lucrative to resist: a yearly salary of $2,500, plus maintenance and transportation expenses, with Oldfield retaining all prize money. It was based on

Winton's policy of "If you can't beat 'em, join 'em," and Barney signed on the dotted line.

"Take it easy with old 999," he warned Cooper. "She's a devil when she busts loose."

"I'll keep her on a tight rein," Tom promised. "And— good luck, Barney."

"Thanks," grinned Oldfield. "I just might need a little."

In August of 1903, when Oldfield joined Winton, several other factories were also engaged in auto racing. Peerless, Stearns, Packard, Oldsmobile and Knox were all in active competition, hoping to prove the durability and speed of their latest models. The Winton Company had received a tremendous boost in prestige late the previous month when the first coast-to-coast trip by automobile had been made by a New England physician, H. Nelson Jackson, at the wheel of a 20-horsepower chain-drive Winton. Jackson had purchased the car for $3,000 from a private owner and set out from San Francisco on May 23, headed for New York City. Since the first mile of concrete highway was not to be completed until 1908, it was an impossibly rugged journey. The Winton bounced over prairies and buffalo wallows, forded bridgeless streams and survived rain, heat, sandstorms and the intense curiosity of gun-toting cowboys, to whom an auto was as strange as a unicorn.

Under the heading "A Real Live Automobile," Oregon's *Lake County Examiner* printed the following account of Jackson's passage: "The way the streets of Lakeview were lined with people Tuesday afternoon one would think a circus was coming to town, or a Fourth of July procession was about to pass. While it was neither, the people's curiosity had been aroused from a report that the first automobile to visit Lake County was coming this way, and that if they wished to see it pass it was necessary to have a place in the front row. . . . It hove into sight at just 4 o'clock after spending six hours on the road from Alturas, 60 miles from here. The crowds surged forward to get a first look at a real live auto, a machine that nine-tenths of the people of Lake County had never seen. . . ."

A block and tackle was needed to pull the machine free of countless mudholes, while gasoline had to be obtained from local shopkeepers at exorbitant prices. A variety of crippling mechanical ailments delayed the trip, and bewildered town smithies were often called upon to weld an axle or repair broken body sections. On July 26, after more than two months of hardship, the battered mud-daubed Winton puttered into New York, an exhausted Jackson at the wheel.

In track competition, the first Winton Bullet had also set many records, and now the fast Bullet No. 2, with Oldfield up, was expected to further enhance the marque's reputation.

This machine was one of the first cars to utilize an eight-cyclinder in-line engine (achieved by bolting a pair of four-cylinder units together). Two stout frame rails supported the power plant and each side of the low wooden body was covered with aluminum sheeting. A single, high wooden seat was provided for the driver, and the total effect was not unlike a flatboat on wheels.

On August 29, Barney set a new three-mile record with the Bullet at Columbus, Ohio (3:10), then took the car to Grosse Pointe where he won two out of three heats against Cooper's 999.

But the eight-cylinder unit was not performing to Oldfield's satisfaction, and the car was withdrawn from the meet. In the 10-mile Detroit Free-For-All, run on the afternoon of September 9, Barney took over Winton's lighter, four-cylinder "Baby" Bullet. Tires were a major problem in these early days of the sport, lacking cord, with only fabric in the rubber. Treads were nonexistent, and the smooth rubber wore at a savage rate on the rough, choppy dirt tracks. Therefore, by lap 6, the Bullet's rear tires had worn dangerously thin.

Intent on getting by Harry Cunningham's Packard "Gray Wolf," Oldfield ignored the possibility of a blowout and swept past into a full-throttle lead on the seventh lap. He was stretching his advantage when a rear tire suddenly burst, sending the Bullet into a skid. Starter A. J. Picard shouted: "My God, Barney's going into the fence!"

Out of control, the Bullet mashed through the wooden railing, headed diagonally down the bank and swerved to demolish a sizable tree—pitching Oldfield from the driver's seat. He landed on his back, breaking a rib and suffering deep flesh wounds. Frank Shearer, a spectator who had been sitting atop the fence, was fatally injured in the crash. He was dead when medical aid reached him.

Stunned at the news, Barney shook his head. "They

warned people not to sit on the rail," he said. "I was afraid something like this might happen. Why didn't he listen to what they told him?"

Barney later admitted: "I knew it wasn't my fault, but I couldn't get it off my mind. At first I decided to quit racing. But I didn't quit—and the accident didn't affect my nerve, as they so often do."

During his hospitalization, Oldfield was attacked by a motoring journal for "unsafe tactics." Among other charges, the article condemned him for steering the Bullet with one arm on the straightaway past the grandstand while waving to the crowd. Barney penned an angry reply: "I asssure you that I have great strength in my right arm, and am as steady with it as many drivers I know who steer with both arms."

In truth, Barney could not resist acknowledging the cheers of his admirers, and he was rapidly becoming the nation's most talked-about competitor. By October he was back with Bullet 2, setting another world's record in winning the 15-miler at Yonkers, New York, averaging 61.7 mph in what one reporter termed "a spectacle few who witnessed it can ever forget."

Since he'd chipped several molars in the Detroit crash he now drove with a thick cigar stub clenched between his teeth. It served as a protective cushion—and soon became his most famous trademark.

Oldfield took the Bullet to California the following month—establishing three new dirt-track marks in Denver on the way west—and wheeled around the track at

Agricultural Park fast enough to shatter his own mile record.

Barney left nothing to chance, and explained his technique of passing on a dirt oval: "The first thing I do before a race is to watch the way the wind carries the dust. If I see that it holds to the upper turn I do not try to pass a man at that point, but hold to the lower turn where it clears better."

The American Automobile Association (formed in 1902), in its role as the governing body of auto racing under the astute chairmanship of A. R. Pardington, had authorized the east coast of Florida for a prominent week-long speed meeting, beginning in late January of 1904. The affair was held on the 15-mile sweep of Ormond-Daytona's glass-smooth beach, affording drivers the rare opportunity of full-speed motoring. W. K. Vanderbilt and Barney Oldfield shared star billing, and photos of both men were hawked on the sand by energetic pitchmen who received "fifty cents a throw" for Barney's smiling visage.

The Winton Bullet was the only American-made car entered in the contest for the Mile Championship. The first heat went to Vanderbilt's 90-hp German Mercedes; Oldfield took the second, nosing out Vanderbilt in the third and final run to the tape. He went on to capture the initial heat of the Five Mile Championship also, coasting over the finish with a broken crankshaft, which eliminated him from further competition.

As Barney's fame grew, so did his appetite for high,

wide, and handsome living, and the boy from Toledo pulled out all the stops. Now addicted to Havanas, Oldfield ordered his stogies in 2,000-lot boxes, and casually handed out five-dollar tips to wide-eyed waiters and doormen. In San Francisco, after he'd been met at the station by an enthusiastic brass band, he invited all of the sixty-five musicians to be his guests at the famed Palace Hotel. That evening he picked up the tab for $845, leaving a characteristically lavish tip.

The fast thoroughbreds also caught Barney's fancy, and he would often spend all afternoon at tracks such as Ascot, wagering heavily on each race. In an era in which the average family man's annual income ran to $500, Oldfield was spending a fortune every week—and the early farm years in Ohio were washed away in a bubbling tide of imported champagne.

Barroom brawling became another of his avocations, but he was ill-equipped for these alcoholic battles. Possessed of a lion's courage, Barney was unhappily cursed with a jaw of glass, and when his initial punch failed to eliminate an opponent Oldfield usually ended up on the floor, staring at a brass spittoon. Boxing champ James J. Jeffries (who had taken the heavyweight crown away from Bob Fitzsimmons in 1899) was a close pal, and saved Oldfield from many a thrashing. ("I did more fighting in saloons getting old Barney out of scrapes than I ever did in the ring," Jeff later admitted.)

Since he was spending money faster than even he could earn it, Oldfield became desperate. When he failed to honor an eastern race commitment in order to accept a more lucrative offer to compete in Florida, the AAA closed in. Called before chairman Pardington, Barney was given a stern lecture and fined $100. When Alex Winton learned of this he refused to renew Oldfield's contract.

"I won't have scandal connected with the Winton Automobile," he stated angrily. Then his tone softened. "Barney, I think I can understand why you behave the way you do. Overindulgence is often the aftereffect of poverty, but when a man works for me the company *must* come first. I'm afraid you're through driving the Winton Bullet."

"That's just dandy," replied Oldfield. "Lou Mooers has been after me to handle a Peerless for him, and that's exactly what I'm gonna do, come August first when my contract runs out."

6

GIANT ON A GREEN DRAGON

Established in 1869, the Peerless Company had switched from bicycles to horseless carriages by 1900, and maintained a staff of fifty when Louis P. Mooers joined the firm early the following year. His ideas were solid and revolutionary, and within a few months he had supervised the construction of a four-cylinder racing machine which was used as a model for the 1903 Peerless production car (utilizing a drop-center frame to gain a lower center of gravity). Advertisements featured a buxom, smiling Gibson girl draped seductively over the hood of a low-slung Peerless. Under Mooers direction, the company also built the world's first production-model closed car, preceding the rest of the auto industry by a full decade.

When Oldfield arrived on the scene, in mid-1904, Mooers had already built the first of the company's famous "Green Dragons." The racer, originally designed to compete for Ireland's Gordon Bennett Cup, boasted a four-speed gearbox, and engine of "square" bore and stroke (6 by 6), and featured a split shaft drive carrying power directly to each wood-spoked rear wheel. (This replaced the awkward, less efficient chain drive arrangement.)

Barney achieved immediate success with the Dragon, scoring a daredevil victory over Herb Lytle's big eight-cylinder Pope "Tornedo" that August in Buffalo, New York. He then appeared at Grosse Pointe to vanquish eleven rivals, in a winning exhibition that saw him lap the entire field (including Winton's two Bullets—which finished second and third).

Mooers was jubilant. "I've arranged for your entry in the Louisiana Purchase Trophy race at St. Louis," he told Barney. "You're a cinch to win!"

"I want my folks to see the World's Fair," said Oldfield. "Can we take them along?"

Mooers nodded. "Tell 'em to start packing!"

The gala World's Fair in St. Louis was representative of a happily expanding nation. By 1904, under Teddy Roosevelt's second term as President, the electric light, the phonograph, telephone, gas cooking and indoor plumbing were rapidly becoming available to most of the population. The Panama Canal was under way, and New Yorkers were delighted and amazed at their recently completed subway. The Wright brothers had made a successful heavier-than-air flight from Kill Devil Hill at

Kitty Hawk, North Carolina, late in '03, and during the same year the Edison Studios in New Jersey had turned out the first motion picture to tell a story, *The Great Train Robbery*. "Movies" were now a part of America's mass entertainment, sharing the limelight with such popular footlight stars as Will Rogers and George M. "Yankee Doodle" Cohan.

No less a showman than either of these men, Oldfield shrewdly prepared for the big day in St. Louis by ordering an all-new forest green driving suit to match the color of his Peerless. He also donned a special green leather helmet to complete the effect—and the crowds loved it. Thus attired, "as were the daring members of Robin Hood's outlaw band," he lined up the Dragon next to A. C. Webb's big Pope-Toledo on August 28 for the day's main event.

Some 25,000 spectators were on hand on this windy afternoon to witness the speedfest, and Barney was the odds-on favorite. However, both Oldfield and Webb got off to a false start (due to the exceptionally thick dust which obscured the flagman) and immediately became involved in a nose-to-nose open-throttle duel out of the first turn. On the straightaway Webb pulled ahead, with the Dragon right behind him as they thundered into the second turn. At that moment a walnut-sized rock, kicked up by Webb's churning wheels, struck Oldfield in the face, smashing his goggles. Blinded by dust, he plunged through the fence, mowing down seven posts and splintering a hundred feet of rail. His twisted machine came to an abrupt halt against a massive oak, and—as at Grosse

Pointe—Barney was catapulted from the wreckage, all but scalping himself as he grazed a heavy tree limb.

Henry Oldfield was the first to reach the fallen driver and he cradled his son's bleeding head in his lap on the way to a St. Louis hospital. Several spectators had been crowding the fence, and the Dragon had swept through them, killing John Scott, a track employee, and Nathan Montgomery, part-time stable hand. Almost a dozen others were injured, none fatally.

Oldfield himself had narrowly escaped death. In addition to the deep head wound, he sustained a punctured lung, shattered ankle, crushed chest and several broken ribs. First reports on his condition were dire.

Barney's mother, arriving late at the track with a freshly baked chocolate cake she was bringing to her son, heard newboys shouting out the blatant headlines: "Oldfield dead," they chanted. "Daredevil Dean of Racing Drivers dies in crash!" Not until she reached the hospital, breathless and half-crazed with shock, did Sarah discover that her son was still alive.

When Barney awoke the next morning, wrapped in white, a huge vase of flowers confronted him on his bedside table. He blinked at them.

"Who sent those?" he asked the nurse.

"Compliments of Mrs. Holland," the girl replied crisply.

"I don't know any Mrs. Holland. Take the damn things away. They remind me of a funeral."

"You can make that request of the lady herself," said the nurse. "She'll be in to see you this afternoon."

Bess Holland was an attractive, brown-eyed widow who'd been introduced to Barney at a party the day prior to the race under her maiden name of Rebecca Gooby. Instantly attracted to the devil-be-damned Oldfield, she had been watching him at the fairgrounds when the accident occurred.

"The doctor tells me you'll be well again soon," she said to him that afternoon.

Barney grinned. "You promise to nurse me and I'll get well *twice* as fast!"

Barney was then separated permanently from Beatrice, his first wife, and as Bess visited him each day attraction turned to love. When he was allowed to wobble out of the hospital on crutches a week later she was there to steady him—and they were constantly together thereafter. Bess tended his injuries until he felt strong enough to drive again, then proudly declared to the press: "I'm with Barney, body and soul, in everything he undertakes."

Green Dragon No. 2 was a much more powerful 60-hp version of the car Oldfield had demolished at St. Louis, built for speed from its pointed radiator to its driving seat placed directly over the rear axle.

Barney seemed pleased with his new car, although he expressed bitterness over what he termed the "outright bloodthirst" of the crowds who came to watch him drive. (After the St. Louis crash, spectators had torn fiercely at the wreckage of the Dragon—even cutting up the aluminum bonnet for souvenirs.)

"They're like a pack of vultures," he charged in an interview. "They pay to see me drive because they want to be there when something lets go. They want me dead, but I figure to fool 'em and stick around for a while."

On October 15, in Cleveland, Barney met his chief rival, Earl Kiser, for the American Championship: Dragon vs. Bullet. Oldfield won the title in two straight heats, but even in victory his driving was more subdued than it had ever been.

Later that same month, at Brighton Beach, he backed off sharply on the turns, and was soundly beaten by Italian ace Paul Satori and French champion Maurice Bernin.

After the meet he admitted to reporters: "I lost my nerve completely out there. When Bernin got the pole from me in the third mile I was forced to the outer rail and came within an inch of going through the fence. That did it. I guess I was still thinking about St. Louis."

Within a few days Oldfield had shaken off self-doubts, and announced that he would be meeting Bernin and Satori again for the World Championship on October 29 on the Empire City track at Yonkers. "And this time I'll take the turns right up to the point of capsize in order to win," he declared.

"Oldfield To Challenge Death," the papers headlined, revealing the fact that Oldfield had placed $5,000 of his own money on himself and that he had vowed to let nothing keep him from being the first to reach the checkered flag.

High society turned out in force for the event. Pre-race betting favored the European stars, but the hero of Manila, Admiral Dewey (sharing a front row grandstand with the Vanderbilts), personally wagered on Oldfield with the comment: "I'll back an American every time."

However, it seemed the Admiral had little but patriotism to support his judgment, for the field arrayed against Barney's Dragon seemed overwhelming: Leon Thery (victor in the last Gordon Bennett Cup Race) in his winning 80-hp Richard-Brasier; Maurice Bernin in his 90-hp Renault and Italy's Satori in a 90-hp Fiat. All more powerful machines in the capable hands of Europe's racing experts.

But Oldfield was out to redeem himself, and spirit overcame horsepower. Blasting around the turns at record speed, Barney avenged his loss in a dazzling display of dirt-track talent that prompted *The New York Times* to state: "Not only did he entirely outclass his rivals, but he established a new world's record in doing so. (10 miles at 9:12⅗) Oldfield's nerve never faltered as he took the turns with magnificent precision. Facing the throng in the grandstand, he was hailed with loud shouts as the champion automobile driver of the world."

When Thery sailed for home that November he paid his American competitor the ultimate compliment. "Your Mr. Oldfield is absolutely fearless," said the Frenchman.

Now at the pinnacle of success, Barney's name on a contract meant overflow crowds and substantial profits.

The "World's Champion Automobilist" began a whirl-wind tour of the United States and Canada, netting thousands of dollars and international acclaim. Records fell under the Dragon's wheels like leaves in autumn, and by the end of the year Barney held all dirt track marks from one to 50 miles. (During an 18-week period that season he competed at 20 tracks in as many cities, winning every event he entered.) Even bad weather failed to slow him. In Fresno, California, when he learned that a youth had ridden 50 miles on horseback just to see him drive, Barney insisted on taking out the Dragon despite a treacherously muddy track. He set a new record that afternoon: 50 miles in under 50 minutes.

Oldfield the man was gradually being replaced by Oldfield the legend. With an unlit cigar between his teeth, a pair of round racing goggles over his eyes and his dark hair "given to the wind" (as one reporter poet-ically phrased it), he embodied the unconquerable steel-nerved daredevil, providing another idol for Americans to take to their hearts. His famous shout "You know me, Barney Oldfield!" invariably brought forth wild applause —and farm youths who had never seen an auto would yell themselves hoarse as they watched Barney man-handle the growling, flame-spitting Dragon at full throttle around a weed-grown mile horse track. Danger was Oldfield's stock in trade, and his narrow escapes were in the best tradition of dime thrillers.

In November he raced a Southern Pacific train to a crossing, and made it across with scant inches to spare. At San Bernardino, in December, a rear tire exploded upon striking a deep pothole and the Dragon whipped viciously across the dirt, jumped the track, sailed over a six-foot ditch and ploughed to a smoking standstill in a field. Barney was shaken, but unhurt.

And when they asked him why he continued to drive his reply was revealingly honest. "There's just one thing which tempts me to go on risking my neck time and again. I'm a firm believer in the product and I always spell it with a capital *M*—for Money."

By the fall of 1904 Oldfield had formed an alliance that would profitably endure, off and on, for the remainder of his long career. He had taken the redoubtable, rotund promoter, William Hickman Pickens, into his employ. Tom Cooper had sold 999 to Pickens shortly after Barney had joined Winton, and the canny Alabama-born promoter had made the "red hellwagon" pay off handsomely—until his star driver, "Daredevil" Hausman, had been killed in a spectacular crash with the tricky machine. Barney, accompanied by his manager, Ernie Moross, promised to liberate Pickens from a Salt Lake City hotel (by paying his long-overdue room bill) if he'd agree to serve as their "advance agent." The arrangement was made. Will would check on fair dates, visit newspapers, distribute posters and publicity—all of which was necessary in the successful operation of "Oldfield's circus." (The battered 999 was shipped to Los Angeles, but when Pickens discovered that the freight bill amounted to $140 he told the railroad they could keep the car. Many years later, after passing through various hands, 999 ended up in the Henry Ford Museum in Dearborn, Michigan.)

In Reno, Nevada, Barney's appearance was preceded by a newspaper article directly blaming him for the three spectator deaths at Detroit and St. Louis. That same evening, when the Dragon was quartered in the local stable (the town had no garage), three lean cowmen slowly circled the car, examining every inch of metal.

"Well," said the first, "you kin see it ain't true."

"Yup," agreed the second. "If this here Oldfield was on the level they'd be here plain enough. But they ain't."

Pickens, overhearing the conversation, stepped forward. "Just what are you gents looking for?"

"Proof of the killin', that's what," stated the third of the trio. "If Oldfield kilt three critters jes' like the papers say he done then *they'd* be there."

"They?" echoed Pickens, plainly confused. "What are 'they'?"

The first cowman spat into the dust. "Notches, that's what. One fer each killin'!"

And the trio walked away, muttering their disappointment.

For the 1904 world record books, the Oldfield–Peerless combination had chalked up the following marks:

Miles	Time	Average mph
1	00:53	67.92
9	08:04	66.94
10	09:12 ⅖	65.17
25	23:38 ⅗	63.44
50	48:40 ⅕	61.63

By the summer of 1905, with the new century well on its way, America was grooming itself for speed. The flying machine was now a solid (if somewhat unsteady) reality; the first of the great cross-country Glidden Tours was underway—and the latest in ladies' wear featured a chic motoring ensemble including goggles, linen duster, leather gauntlets and a sensible bonnet that laced neatly below milady's chin. (After all, you simply couldn't keep an ostrich-plume hat on your head at 30 miles per hour in your merry Oldsmobile!)

The wacky, wonderfully wicked world of high society captured most of the headlines in '05 (with lavish dinners served on horseback, banquet rooms filled with nightingales supplied by a local zoo and the introduction of a titled Prince who turned out to be a monkey in full evening regalia), but "Never-look-back" Oldfield's name still garnered its generous share of news space; his hairbreadth escapes continued to make the front pages.

A real wheel collapsed in Connecticut; his car spun into the ocean at Ormond Beach; a blowout pitched him through the fence in Chicago . . . and, on August 9, at a meet in Detroit, Barney's Dragon violently hooked wheels with Dan Worgis's Reo "Redbird." The *Free-Press* reported: ". . . a cloud of dust, a sickening crash, and the form of the daring Oldfield was seen to hurtle through the air. A cry of horror burst forth from the stands, intermingled with the shrieks of women who swooned from the sight. . . ."

Thrown some 20 feet from the wrecked Peerless, Barney was still firmly grasping the uprooted steering wheel when help reached him.

The paper quoted Oldfield from Harper's Hospital: "In a way I'm glad the old Dragon has been put out of business. We've seen some good times together, and she still holds the records all right, but she was just a little slow for the cars of today. Webb Jay beat me fair yesterday in his Steamer, but he'll have to go some to have anything on me when I get back on the dirt. I'll be going fast miles before the month is over!"

Barney's only injury in the Detroit crash had been a moderate scalp wound, but his chief dirt-track rivals, Earl Kiser and Webb Jay, were far less fortunate in subsequent accidents. Just a week later, in Cleveland, Kiser smashed up the Winton Bullet, severely mangling his left leg. It had to be amputated. To aid the stricken driver, Oldfield staged a benefit race in Dayton—the entire proceeds of over $2,600 went to Kiser.

By mid-September, after losing control of his famous White Steamer, "Whistling Billy," on a Buffalo track, Webb Jay lay crushed in a New York hospital. He had broken 27 bones and suffered a brain concussion, and these injuries were to keep him bedridden for a full year.

"I think it is probable that some of the more daring fellows like Oldfield will keep on racing," he told pressmen, "but the game is so dangerous I fear it is a dead one."

Barney was badly shaken by these incidents, and he told Pickens that after the season ended he planned to change occupations. "I'm quitting while I'm still in one piece," he vowed. "Hell, I've got talent and I've got a name. I intend to put 'em both to work for me—in vaudeville." He grinned and slapped Pickens on the back. "Old son, we're going into show business!"

7

FROM BROADWAY TO BRIARCLIFF

The automobile invaded the Broadway stage in 1902, when a frightened crook employed a malfunctioning horseless carriage to effect his escape during a sleazy musical comedy entitled *Beauty and the Beast*. Theatergoers were fascinated by the appearance of an "infernal contraption" on the boards and a trend was quickly established. By September of 1907 no less than eleven principal characters, in as many concurrently running Broadway plays, made their entrances in automobiles.

Oldfield had taken the popularity of the auto into careful account when he moved into the world of grease paint, and with the aid of Will Pickens he'd worked out a "sure-fire act." Behind the footlights, two genuine racing machines would engage in what appeared to be a fierce, wheel-to-wheel race. A pair of treadmills and some rapidly moving background scenery would provide the thrills. Barney, of course, would inevitably be the victor, dramatically forging ahead of the opposing vehicle (as treadmill speed was decreased) on the final lap.

Since no vacant theaters were available for perfecting this act, rehearsals were held between midnight and dawn at a playhouse just a few blocks from Broadway. Oldfield, who preferred to pursue other pleasures after dark, reluctantly accepted the emergency arrangement— but only after Pickens had solemnly assured his client that he possessed "an amazing natural acting ability," and was surely headed for a magnificent stage career.

After a week of tedious all-night sessions, even the indefatigable Pickens was exhausted. He called the rehearsal to an early halt with a suggestion that they adjourn to the Astor Hotel for a nightcap. Oldfield instantly endorsed this proposal.

At the Astor bar they encountered the fabulous man-about-Manhattan "Diamond Jim" Brady, an old friend of Barney's. When Jim heard about their vaudeville plans he slapped the counter with a jewel-encrusted fist.

"Hell, I have got me one great idea!"

"And what is that?" asked Oldfield.

"Go see Charlie Dillingham at the Broadway. He's got a play in rehearsal over there that's ready-made for you. He'll grab your act for the show and you'll get more money than a stint in vaudeville would ever pay you!"

"Sounds fine!" said Pickens.

"I'm sold," Barney agreed. "Only one thing—I gotta see my name in lights."

Dillingham's play, *The Vanderbilt Cup*, dealt with the wild auto race which, in just two years, had become an annual American classic.

Run over twenty-eight miles of narrow, high-crowned road in Nassau County, Long Island, for the cup donated by W. K. Vanderbilt, the first affair, in October of '04, had been won by George Heath in a French Panhard. The '05 follow-up was taken by Victor Hemery in a Darracq. Both contests were plagued by numerous crashes and narrow escapes as crowds spilled into the roadways—and had therefore received tremendous publicity.

Producer Dillingham had wisely decided to combine the excitement of this international auto race with the services of a great American stage personality, Elsie Janis. The result was a musical drama, *The Vanderbilt Cup*—and Diamond Jim's suggestion was perfectly timed. Barney was hired immediately, with a guarantee of star billing.

Two racing cars were used in each performance: Barney in his Dragon and Tom Cooper at the wheel of a Peerless Blue Streak. Cooper, who had also retired from the speedpaths, hugely enjoyed the chance to recreate the excitement of a motor duel on stage, and threw himself into the new venture with immense enthusiasm.

The play opened in mid-January of 1906, and Broadway critics received it warmly. "The big effect comes in the second act," wrote the New York *American,* "when Barney Oldfield, the famous driver and his Green Dragon racer that holds every record in auto circles from one mile to fifty, is introduced in a contest with another machine driven by his long-time sidekick, Tom Cooper. The giants are seen together on the stage traveling at a lively clip, spitting flame and sparks while the roar of exhausts fairly shakes the building." The New York *World* declared: "These racing machines rock and roar and spit blue fire, enough to shake the gold fillings out of one's teeth, while the scenery whizzes by at a mile a minute. Yea, verily! As a sporting thriller this Cup contest has the chariot race of Ben-Hur beaten to a frazzle."

During one performance Barney arranged to have buckets of dirt poured from overhead onto the treadmill in order to provide more "atmosphere." He proudly stated that "it was doggone realistic. That audience coughed for a week!"

Although Barney was earning $2,000 a month for his brief stint, he was not satisfied. Many of his boxing pals had taken to the stage, flexing their vocal cords as well as their biceps. Jeffries essayed the role of Davy Crockett, while Bob Fitzsimmons played a bewigged Frank Merriwell in *The Village Blacksmith,* and "Gentleman Jim" Corbett starred as *A Naval Cadet.* Even old John L. Sullivan, the bare-knuckle king, donned grease paint to sneer his way through *Uncle Tom's Cabin* in the role of Simon Legree. It was all too much for Oldfield's competitive ego.

"I gotta have some lines," he told Dillingham. "How's about giving me a chance to *act?*"

Informed that all the speaking parts were filled, Barney began pestering Hugh Ford, the stage manager, for a chance to emote. Driven to despair, Ford beckoned to the frustrated thespian at a special rehearsal. "We're adding a new scene," he said, "and I can use you in it. When I give the word you come in from the wings with a plate, smile and say: 'Here's the ham.' Okay?"

"Bernhardt had to start small," said Oldfield. "So gimme the plate."

As the scene progressed, and he was not called, Barney grew impatient standing in the wings. "Do I carry out the ham now?" he finally yelled to Ford.

"No," the stage manager replied acidly, unable to resist the opening. "You merely make the confession."

One of Barney's proudest possessions was a spirited Irish terrier called "Hypo." Each day after lunch Oldfield and Hypo took a walk together, and on one of these casual strolls, of a Saturday afternoon, Barney was angrily accosted by a tall stranger.

"Why don't you take that crummy mutt of yours to another neighborhood?" he demanded.

"Because I happen to live in *this* neighborhood," Oldfield replied.

Sensing trouble, Hypo growled.

The stranger, in angry frustration, lashed out with a heavy foot, planting his shoe squarely on Hypo's rump.

Barney instantly retaliated by knocking the stranger

down with a powerfully delivered blow to the chin.

The tall man, eyes clouded in fury, reached into his coat. A long-barreled weapon glinted in his right hand.

"Run, Hypo!" shouted Barney. "He's got a gun!"

Man and dog sprinted for safety as the stranger brandished his weapon.

"I've learned one thing," Barney told a reporter sent to investigate the bizarre incident. "Auto racing is a whole lot safer than walking your dog!"

The Vanderbilt Cup took to the road, after ten weeks in New York, and Barney went along. He was on tour with the show in April when San Francisco's devastating earthquake and fire stunned the nation.

"This San Francisco business shook me up," he wrote in a letter to a friend in Toledo. "I can't go on living a fake life on the stage. I belong back in the real world and that's where I'm headed."

In late May, with the Dragon, Barney won the 50-mile main event in Lexington, Kentucky. His theatrical career was over.

Oldfield's divorce from Beatrice became final on November 16—and just three days later Tom Cooper was killed when his car overturned on the streets of New York. Barney sadly attended the funeral, and for weeks thereafter could not rid himself of the vision of his old friend laid to rest in a flower-draped coffin.

"I keep dreaming about Tom," he wrote his parents that December, "and each time I see him as he was when

I looked upon his dead body—always thin and white, with that big scar on his face."

By the end of the month, however, he forced the unhappy memory from his mind as he prepared for his second marriage.

Bess and Barney were wed in January of 1907. A New York columnist described Oldfield's new bride as "a striking, brown-eyed brunette who is a talented artist and musician. Raised in California, she married the late M. O. Holland when she was quite young . . . Bess loves excitement, and her new life should provide plenty."

On their honeymoon Barney took his bride to the horse races, and she became a devoted follower of "the fast nags" when a four-legged "Barney Oldfield" galloped to a successive series of wins at Ascot Park in Los Angeles. (The newlyweds reportedly earned $1,500 betting on Barney's namesake in four starts there.)

Able to command up to $3,000 for a single afternoon's appearance with the 90-hp Dragon No. 3, Oldfield easily amassed enough to buy this car and the Blue Streak from the factory when his contract with Peerless expired that season. He outfitted a special railroad car to transport the two racers, setting out for the southern fair circuit.

However, despite the fact that he had no income tax with which to contend, Barney spent money faster than he could make it. He packed $10,000 in jewels with him when he traveled, sporting a four-carat diamond ring on his little finger and a pearl-and-ruby stickpin in his tie. His $1,000 sealskin floor-length overcoat became the talk of Detroit. Between driving chores he took Bess to the races, hunted quail, entered bowling marathons (one of which lasted a full 24 hours) and was host to gigantic champagne parties attended by the elite of the sports world. As the New York columnist had predicted, Bess Oldfield was getting plenty of excitement from her fast-paced life with auto racing's "human comet." In fact, at Portland, Oregon, she got a bit more than even she had bargained for.

This incident involved Oldfield's pride. Ernie Moross had set up a race meet at Irvington Park, just outside Portland, over the Fourth of July weekend, but due to heavy rains, only two of the nine scheduled events were run. When several dozen fans demanded their money back Moross refused. This led to a charge of fraud, leveled at Oldfield and his manager—and a court appearance was ordered for July 7.

"I've always played square with my public," Oldfield swore. "I'm deeply hurt by this charge."

On the evening of July 6, free on $500 bail and despondent over the pending court action, Barney began to drink. When he staggered drunkenly into his room at 2 A.M. on the third floor of the Portland Hotel, Bess berated him for his weakness.

"I'll show you how weak I am," he snarled, and abruptly smashed out the terrace windows with both fists. Still raging, he climbed unsteadily out onto the ledge. Bess screamed, grabbing for his coat as he swayed dizzily above the street. Joseph Resing, the house detective, heard her cries for help and rushed into the room, pulling Barney from the ledge.

A chastened Oldfield, both hands bandaged, stood before the judge that afternoon. In a low voice he explained his actions as "those of an intoxicated man," and reiterated his innocence regarding the fiasco at Irvington. The judge nodded when Barney had finished speaking.

"Mr. Oldfield, I believe you're telling me the truth. There is no evidence to support the charge placed against you." He rapped his gavel sharply against the desk. "Case dismissed."

By early spring of 1908 Barney had sold both of the Peerless racers, and announced to the press that he had given up the auto game: "If I could get together in one chunk all of the real estate I've breathed into my lungs, swallowed, dug out of my ears, rubbed off my face and brushed off my clothes since I've been driving the dirt, I could stick a lovely mile track right out in the middle of Lake St. Clair!"

Yet the newsprint proclaiming Oldfield's retirement was barely dry on the page when Harlan Whipple, president of the AAA, offered Barney a brutish 90-hp Stearns for the season. It was the kind of deal Oldfield couldn't resist and, by late April, at the Briarcliff Road Races in New York, he was back in his familiar crouch behind the taped wheel.

Although he had long since mastered the circular tracks, open road racing, with its twists, sudden turns and engine-killing straightaways, was totally new to Barney and he did not fare well at Briarcliff over a course in which 30 miles were consumed each lap. Oldfield was officially credited with 11th place after several off-the-road excursions with the heavy Stearns. This race *was* notable, however, in that it marked the debut of a young Italian-American daredevil who was to become Barney's chief rival and one of the sport's great champions, Ralph De Palma.

In the fall of the previous year 24-year-old De Palma had gone to work for the Allen-Kingston plant as an assembler, graduating to the job of personal mechanic for company driver Al Campbell. Ralph had been racing cycles professionally since 1902, but now wanted to try his skill with the faster four-wheelers. He got his chance at Briarcliff when Campbell was unlucky enough to break a leg in practice; De Palma promptly took over the Allen-Kingston, ending in a ditch with a twisted front axle after just four laps. Yet from this unimpressive beginning he went on to achieve the status of a true giant.

8

SPEED KING OF THE WORLD

In 1908 the working man's dream was forged into solid steel by Henry Ford when he produced the 20-hp four-cylinder Model T, a truly remarkable machine which revolutionized the auto industry. The supremacy of the horse had ended. For the modest sum of $825 the "common laborer" could own a tough, perky, high-bellied Model T which stubbornly defied mud, snow, gumbo and potholes. It navigated hogback country roads, bounced across fields, clawed up steep hills and refused to say die.

More than 11,000 of Ford's ungainly creations were sold that first year, and (says Rudolph Anderson) "the Model T won for Henry Ford the greatest private fortune ever to be earned from any business and made his name a household word that outdazzled Rockefeller, Carnegie or Edison."

Thanks to the car the nation affectionately called "Tin Lizzie," motoring could no longer be considered the exclusive province of the rich.

Automotive competition continued to make headlines, but (as writer Franklin D. Walker put it) "what the industry needed was a spectacular event designed to prove conclusively that an automobile could hang together long enough to deliver its driver and passengers to just about any destination. It had to be a daring departure from anything ever before tried in motoring."

The New York-to-Paris race was just such an event. Jointly sponsored by the Paris *Le Matin* and *The New York Times*, this 22,000-mile affair over three quarters of the globe was deemed "preposterous, ridiculous, foolhardy and downright impossible." From a Times Square starting point in the dead of winter, the route embraced the northern States, Alaska, the Bering Strait, Siberia and eastern Europe—ending in the French capital.

After the announcement was made, *The New York Times* found itself in the embarrassing position of having no American entry to pit against the European machines (three from France: a De Dion, a Motobloc and a Sizaire; an Italian Zust; and a German Protos). No American manufacturer wanted to risk a car over such a rigorous terrain. However, racing veteran Montague Roberts, then working as a demonstrator for Thomas in New York, prevailed upon his employer, Harry S. Houpt, to place a "Flyer" in the lists.

The carefully prepared De Dion (carrying no less than

seven separate fuel tanks) was favored by many to win, and was to be driven by the swashbuckling Norwegian Arctic explorer, Captain Hans Henrik Hansen, whose curling dragoon mustache added to his already flamboyant character. Hansen had insisted on lashing a mast to the radiator "to take full advantage of a heavy wind astern in the Arctic regions," and boasted that he had done "considerable land sailing in the north."

The massive Protos (6,000 pounds) was also a feared contender, with 176 gallons of gasoline aboard and a crew of three German army officers "especially trained for automobiling." They packed a small arsenal of guns on board and appeared to look upon the race as a military conquest.

Roberts' Thomas Flyer was a stock 1907 60-hp model, but the list of non-stock extras included a pair of 14-foot metal-reinforced planks, block and tackle, pick, shovel, ax, hatchet, crowbars, wire cutters, blowtorch, soldering iron, several wrenches of varying size, rifles, acetylene gas, searchlight, foot pump, tire tools, funnel, jack, spare wheels and casings, thermometers, barometers, compass, sextant, water bottles, "grub" kits, tent cloth, chains—and, as Roberts added, "strong backs, stout muscles and hopeful hearts."

The fragile Motobloc was not taken too seriously, and the Sizaire broke down quite early in the going. The Italian Zust, however, proved a solid threat over the initial stages of the long contest.

Roberts set the pace into Buffalo, breaking trail through heavy snow. The De Dion and the Zust joined the Thomas for a three-car duel, but the American entry pulled away, leading its foreign rivals by a full day upon reaching Chicago.

The struggle continued, despite incredibly savage weather. As Roberts later described it: "We plowed through fields and over roads which were no more than wagon tracks filled with dips, rocks and furrows. Snow and rain turned them into quagmires, and we were continually subjected to below-freezing temperatures."

In Wyoming the crew of the Zust found themselves ambushed by a growling pack of half-starved timber wolves, and after shooting some two dozen of the ferocious animals the Italians made good their escape.

Mechanic-driver George Schuster took over the wheel of the Thomas at Cheyenne (since Roberts had to return east due to a personal commitment) and motored into San Francisco still leading the race. The Flyer had required 41⅓ days to cross the continent from New York. The De Dion was second, with the Motobloc entirely out of the running. The Zust and Protos had not yet arrived.

The race across the frozen wastes of Siberia saw the Protos move up to challenge Schuster's Thomas, as the De Dion was withdrawn. The Germans finally reached the finish line in Paris four days ahead of the American entry, but the celebration in Berlin was short-lived since an official ruling placed the Protos in second. (The car was penalized 30 days for traveling by train from Pocatello, Idaho, to Seattle and avoiding Alaska.)

The Thomas was declared winner, having covered a total of 13,431 land miles as well as almost 7,000 at sea.

The Homeric battle had lasted from mid-February until late July, and had conclusively proven that a well-driven, properly equipped automobile could overcome every conceivable type of road hazard.

This victory brought great honor to America, and garnered the respect of Europe as well as the personal congratulations of Teddy Roosevelt.

On June 17, while the amazing New York-to-Paris battle was still being fought, Oldfield was engaged in three heat races at the Readville track in Massachusetts with Ralph De Palma. In the first of these heats Barney managed to bring his Stearns in ahead of Ralph's Allen-Kingston, but lost the second to the young Italian novice and could do no better in the runoff, with De Palma scoring a decisive victory in his first dirt track event.

Furious with himself over his poor showing, Barney stormed off the track without bothering to congratulate the sensitive De Palma. Thus, without any direct violence, a feud was precipitated between the two drivers which persisted, in varying degree, throughout their careers.

Oldfield capped the '08 season with a first place finish in a 50-miler at Brighton Beach, New York, then entered the round-the-clock, 24-hour endurance race there, taking sixth over-all with co-driver J. B. Marquis in the Stearns. (As a demonstration of the severe tire wear incurred in these early-day contests it is to be noted that one driver, Louis Strang, changed no less than 41 casings on his Renault in 17 hours at Brighton Beach.)

Barney landed back on the front pages with his daredevil antics that winter when he indulged in what was apparently becoming one of his favorite forms of illegal recreation: racing steam locomotives. In this instance, realizing at the last moment that he would not be able to make the grade crossing ahead of a fast-charging freight, he quickly swerved back in the direction in which the train was traveling. Yet the gap was so narrow that his two right wheels rode up and over the side of the locomotive's protruding cowcatcher, almost upsetting his car.

Ed Apperson, one of the auto industry's pioneers, and the man behind the Apperson "Jackrabbit," a famous car of this period, was honestly envious of Oldfield's record in competition. When he learned that Barney had entered a Stearns in the Pasadena Hill Climb that year he determined to design a car which would bring him victory.

The annual event always drew an impressive turnout, since it was acknowledged to be a "real car-tester." The buying public eyed the affair with intense interest.

Apperson detailed the preparation behind his bid: "I designed and built a new five-by-five four-cylinder motor for this '09 running. Now, the Europeans were still ahead of us in many respects, and I knew that the French carburetor was superior to anything we had on this side of the water. Friend of mine was working as a chauffeur, handling a French car, so one Sunday I asked for a close look-see under the hood. I examined the carburetor real careful, then went home to my shop and built one just like it. Then, after I had my engine perking sweet for me, I put on special 30-inch wheels in front and 34-inchers in the rear, and I was set."

Ed described a particularly tricky section of the course: "Our route went right through the Pasadena city streets, and in one place we had to cross a raised wooden bridge over some sunken streetcar tracks. Drivers always slowed down for it, because they were afraid not to. Man could snap a front axle like a twig over this stretch. Since I knew the race would be close I figured that if I didn't slow down I'd have the edge I needed to win. So I built my axles out of alloy steel, the first ever used on a U. S. gas-driven car. I'd broken enough front-axle spindles, and I didn't aim to break another when I hit that bridge."

Nothing was left to chance in Apperson's single-minded determination to beat Oldfield; he spent an entire month in Pasadena touring the course, perfecting his technique on each turn and grade.

On race morning, as predicted, crowds overflowed the streets, and Ed felt obliged to warn a patrolman stationed at one of the tightest curves. "You're standing outside the curb," Apperson told him. "Now you better get *inside* when you see me coming, because I'll run right over you if you don't. Either that or I'd have to try and dodge you and end up slamming smack into the crowd—so watch out for me!"

Apperson described the event itself: "It was a race against the clock, with just one of us allowed out on the course at a time, and the result was telephoned back to the line before the next man started. That way, we knew what we had to beat.

"Barney was there with his big Stearns six-cylinder job. He was always a cocky cuss, and he yelled over when he saw me pull up in my four-cylinder job. 'Hi, Ed. How do you expect to win in a little thing like that?' I told him this wasn't his day, that he'd have to settle for second, and he just shook his head at me like I was crazy.

"Well, we kept on jawing and finally Barney got sore. 'You can't outrun me,' I warned him, 'so there's no use getting all steamed up.'

"'Like hell I can't,' says Barney, and he pulls out a thick roll of bills. 'I got a thousand right here that says I'll beat your time.'

"I didn't want to take his money, but he bellowed like a steer, so we finally made the bet. Now, the start of the climb was a long, slightly downhill straightaway—and I started off in second gear and held it until I came out of the first turn, where I shifted into high without releasing the clutch. I kept my foot on the throttle, even when I saw that wooden bridge coming at me. When I hit it I took off like a bird. Later an old pal of mine, Judge Frederickson of Beverly Hills, paced the distance between where the rear wheels left the ground and where they touched again. It was 88 feet.

"I still had that tight curve to make, and I saw that the crowd had cleared well back from the curb, but that dumb cop still stood there in the street. I waved and hollered, but he didn't see me till the last second, when he suddenly dived out of my way. At that, I ran over his toes!

"Turned out I won the climb by 10 seconds, and Barney handed over his thousand. But he didn't seem surprised at the time I made. In fact, he admitted afterwards that when he saw me cover the first thousand feet of road he knew he was losing a dollar a foot."

Despite this loss to Apperson, Barney's passion for the personal wager remained undiminished. His next bet involved the popular competitor "Smiling George" Robertson who had won the 1908 Vanderbilt Cup in a special $20,000 Locomobile. Since this represented the first American victory in the rugged road classic, newspapermen had plied the cheerful winner with questions. Was it rough?

"Sure was," he replied. "For one thing, you've got to be thick in the shoulders and legs to stand the strain. The steering ratio is almost one-to-one and it takes plenty of muscle to turn the wheel. Then there's the 110 pounds of pressure on the clutch pedal. After pushing that down every minute or so for four hours you end up walking sideways!"

When several papers referred to Robertson as "the nation's greatest driver," Oldfield became annoyed. During a train trip with the Vanderbilt winner, Barney challenged Robertson's right to the title.

"I figure I *am* the best," asserted George. "Since the Cup everybody says so."

The train had pulled into a small town for a routine

stop, and Oldfield noted that Robertson was facing away from the window.

"Bet you a hundred bucks, cash in hand, that the porter would pick me as the best."

"You're on," nodded George. "Call him over."

The Pullman porter was summoned, and Barney edged back from the window, making sure that the fellow could get a clear view of the station platform.

"Now, son," began Oldfield, "I want you to tell us who the world's greatest driver is. Can you do that?"

"Yes, sir!" The porter beamed, exposing a trio of shining gold teeth. "Mr. Barney Oldfield is."

Robertson paid the bet as the train slowly got under way.

"Better take a look behind you, George," grinned Oldfield, pocketing the money.

The big man turned angrily to observe a large billboard near the station platform. It featured a picture of a charging race car under which were the words: "FIRESTONE TIRES ARE MY ONLY LIFE INSURANCE," SAYS BARNEY OLDFIELD, THE WORLD'S GREATEST DRIVER.

Although Oldfield began the 1909 season by campaigning in a National "Old Glory" (named after the American flag he'd painted on the long hood), he soon acquired a $4,000 120-hp German Benz. (This was the same machine Victor Hemery had driven into second place in the 1906 French Grand Prix.)

Barney's first important outing with the Benz was at Indianapolis, when he joined an all-star field (including

Louis Chevrolet, "Wild Bob" Burman, Strang, Lytle, and De Palma) for a series of inaugural events which marked the official opening of the new Speedway.

Carl Fisher had repeatedly stated that the country needed a special track, other than the standard dirt horse ovals, on which to race and test high-performance automobiles. Three other businessmen, Frank Wheeler, James A. Allison and A. C. Newby, joined him in a plan to provide just such a track. They decided to build it some four miles from the center of Indianapolis on a 328-acre tract purchased for this purpose. By mid-August, the tar and crushed stone surfacing was completed on the big 2.5-mile oval, and the popular starter, Fred "Pa" Wagner, was brought to Indiana to flag away the field in the three-day speedfest.*

Barney throttled the Benz to a new American track record when he officially covered the mile in 43.1 seconds (83.5 mph). In the 10-mile Free-For-All he led brilliantly with the German machine until engine trouble allowed Len Zengel to win with his Chadwick. On the final day, with 40,000 fans urging him on, Oldfield not only established a new kilometer record in a solo run, but went on to win the 25-mile Remy Brassard event against De Palma's Fiat and Zengel's Chadwick. The *Automobile Trade Journal* reported: "Oldfield smashed into small fragments the world's records for five, ten, fifteen, twenty and twenty-five miles . . ."

However, at this point, the Speedway's surface had disintegrated under the heavy wheels of the competing

---

* This was just two years before the first of the famous 500-mile classics.

cars, and high speed became a deadly gamble. Switching to the cockpit of his National, Barney was running fifth in the meet's big race for the Wheeler-Schebler trophy, when local favorite Charles Merz blew a tire on the sandpaper-rough south turn, plunging into the crowd. Two spectators and Merz's riding mechanic died in the accident—and the race was subsequently called off. (That same month resurfacing work was begun, and 3,200,000 bricks were used to pave the entire oval, giving the Speedway its famous nickname: "The Brickyard.")

In December Barney hit the Lone Star State and unlimbered the Benz in the teeth of a howling Texas windstorm. Wrapped in an engulfing fur coat with thick mittens and a woolen cap to combat the penetrating cold, he roared over an icy track surface in Dallas to a decisive win, unofficially breaking his own 50-mile record. At the finish line, just in front of the main grandstand, Will Pickens saw to it that Oldfield's hands were dramatically pried loose from their "frozen" position on the steering wheel (choosing to ignore the fact that Barney had waved cheerfully to the crowd on the final lap). His fans loved it.

The newly strengthened AAA (having combined forces with the Automobile Club of America) did not find Oldfield so amusing. When he signed to compete in Atlanta, and ended up driving elsewhere in Georgia that weekend for a larger cash guarantee, Barney found himself again suspended from all AAA-sanctioned events. He was forced to plead his case personally—promising faithfully to obey AAA rules—before the suspension was lifted (although this was by no means his last disagreement with the governing organization).

Off the tracks, Bess was finding her husband equally hard to manage. "He's a devil with the ladies," she admitted. "But I guess you can't expect a man like Barney to sit in front of a living room fire in his slippers!"

Certainly Oldfield was living up to his reputation as a prime hell-raiser. Scheduled to drive at a meet in Missouri, he disappeared for three full days. Will Pickens and Bess made the rounds of every saloon and gambling emporium in Kansas City, finally locating Barney at a dive on Main Street. He was out cold—and they put him on a stretcher and carried him to a taxi.

The following morning, nursing a colossal hangover, Oldfield drove his car straight through the fence on the first turn.

"I made a damn fool of myself out there," he told Bess at dinner that evening. "Few more stunts like this and no decent driver will take me seriously. Trouble is, I'm getting bored. I need to go after something really big."

"Just what *is* on your mind, Barney?"

He looked up defiantly. "The world's land-speed record. I want to go after it—crack it wide open."

"But didn't Marriott's Steamer reach almost 128 miles an hour at Daytona?" Bess asked him. "How could you possibly match him? You haven't got a car capable of that kind of speed."

"There's only one machine to do the job, the one Hemery drove at Brooklands last year—the Lightning Benz,"

Barney told her. "The factory has it on display in New York right now, and with the right kind of luck *that's* the next car I'll own."

With the aid of Ernie Moross the deal was made. Barney traded in his 120-hp Benz and $6,000 cash to get the massive white record-breaker, and when he announced that the car was being shipped directly to Daytona his goal was obvious: Oldfield would try for a new straightaway mark in excess of the 127.5 mph established by Fred Marriott's Stanley Steamer in 1906.

The "Blitzen" Benz was a 21.5-liter chain-driven, overhead-valved monster housing 200 horses under its long bullet snout. The giant four-cylinder engine of 1,312 cubic inches was cast in two blocks, and power was governed by a four-speed transmission.

After a warm-up ride in the big machine next to Barney as he powered over the long stretch of Daytona beach, Bess Oldfield breathlessly stated: "The sand pricks your face like a thousand needles; the sky unwinds above like a big blue sheet of flame and the sea whirls past beside you while your heart stops dead still . . . Sometimes I think it takes an insane man to break the natural laws that my husband breaks when he is after a new world's record."

On the afternoon of March 16, after several trial runs, Barney inserted his cotton earplugs, pulled down his goggles and buried a fresh cigar stub in the corner of his mouth. Then he nodded to the timers. "Okay, boys, this is the one that counts. Me and the Blitzen here—we're gonna warm up the sand a little."

Barney acknowledged the starting signal and the monster Benz began to roll over the hard-packed beach. More throttle, and the car picked up speed, rapidly gaining momentum until (in the awed words of one official observer) "Oldfield was a blur of motion, lost in belching exhaust flame and smoke. Almost before the overtaxed mechanism of the eye had adjusted itself to the changing perspective of his approach he was already past and dwindling in the distance."

Now the big Benz was nudging 100, then it was roaring over the sand at 110 . . . 120 . . . 125. Marriott's mark was smashed as the German charger swept past the timing stand in a sulphurous rush for a new world's land-speed record: 131.7 mph.

"Barney Oldfield Speed King of the World," proclaimed the headlines. "In Blur of Flame Breaks Every Human Record." The *Florida Times Union* summed up his startling achievement: "The speed attained was the fastest ever traveled by a human being, no greater speed having been recorded except that made by a bullet."

Even Kaiser Wilhelm was impressed. He sent Barney a personal wire: I CONGRATULATE A DARING YANKEE ON SO REMARKABLE A PERFORMANCE IN A GERMAN CAR.

Oldfield graphically described his record run: "I let the great machine have its head, and for fully a third of the distance the wheels were off the ground while I fought for control. The front wheels were shooting up and down in a weird dance, and I knew that if a tire

100

burst I would be beyond mortal help. I shot through space until all before me became enshrouded in a dark haze and I approached the verge of unconsciousness. Then I shut her down, knowing I had traveled faster than any other human on the face of the earth."

Reporters scurried, notepads in hand, to Barney's mother. Sarah Oldfield shook her gray head over the news: "He isn't a speed king to me, you know. He's still my baby. And I'm just scared to death every minute he is racing. He tells me 'Don't worry, Mom, I'll come back.' But in my heart there is always the fear that he won't come back. The picture of Barney as a little boy comes into my mind, and sometimes I get it all tangled up with the grown man that the whole world knows. Like I told you—he isn't a speed king to me, he's just my baby still."

To celebrate his achievement properly, Barney began a bar-by-bar blitz that evening which rocked the Florida coast. "By ten o'clock that night," declared a newspaperman, "all the bartenders in town were rubbing their wrists with Mustang Liniment to relieve the soreness caused by teasing the corks out of cold quarts."

Inevitably, Oldfield got into his usual brannigan. On this particular occasion it took a doctor four hours to sew the great man's scalp back on his head. Arriving at his hotel, turbaned in white, Barney encountered a pal in the lobby.

"Migawd, Barney, ya gotta stop this awful fightin'," he warned. "It's too damn dangerous."

"You're absolutely right," agreed the Speed King, his face solemn beneath the bandages. "It'll be only a matter of time when, deep in my cups, I will lick some poor devil so bad he'll die. Then—heaven forbid—they'll hang me!"

And he headed unsteadily for the elevator.

Before leaving Daytona a week later Oldfield added the flying kilometer to his laurels (at 17.4) with the huge Benz, then loaded the machine aboard his special railroad car (now bearing the legend: BARNEY OLDFIELD— SPEED KING) and headed for Venice, California, for a scheduled match race with Ralph De Palma.

The two rivals had dueled each other to a standoff that February in New Orleans, and Barney was anxious to field the Benz against De Palma's giant Fiat at the new Playa del Rey board track.

This was the first of the mighty plank saucers which would eventually replace the dirt tracks, and it had been built by the sportsman Jack Prince. Three million feet of Oregon fir had been used in constructing the mile saucer, and it was banked for high speed—20 degrees all round, with its top rail some 25 feet above the ground. The surface was coated with crushed shells in order to provide proper traction on the steep wooden banking— and both De Palma and Oldfield set new records here. However, their match race was called off when Ralph's Fiat developed mechanical trouble, and the Italian ace was replaced by a young Pasadena amateur, Caleb Bragg, a millionaire who raced for "the fun of it all." He defeated Barney in two straight heats, nosing out the Benz by a few feet at the wire. Oldfield had not yet mastered the powerful German racer on the boards, and it was plain to track observers that he had been competing "on half-throttle."

(After Daytona Barney had admitted to Pickens and Moross that the Blitzen was capable of 150, if properly tuned, but that this rate of speed was "suicidal.")

Returning to the Indianapolis Speedway in late May, Barney won a "Baby" Overland roadster, with special gold-plated fittings, for setting the fastest mile at the meet. He gave this prize to his wife, and for months thereafter Bess proudly drove the special Overland over Detroit streets.

In June, Barney appeared in Kansas City, Missouri, to help publicize the run of the Star Cup Pathfinder (a Stevens-Duryea "Big 6" driven by M. C. Nolan) and stayed on to win several events at Elm Ridge. Three months later, at the Minnesota State Fairgrounds, he clipped De Palma's mile record by a fifth of a second. Asked for a statement, Oldfield grinned. "Well, I figure I might have made it another hundredth of a second faster but for the dead weight of my cheroot."

Reporters followed Barney from town to town; children ran alongside his cars as they were being towed to the local tracks, shouting for autographs; small boys on wooden scooters imitated his swagger with candy cigars and makeshift goggles; crowds chanted his name. Local newspapers outdid one another in luridly describing his heart-stopping performances.

A typical account: "Oldfield shot into the turn with the

wheel of his mighty motor car gripped as no other man can hold it. There was a fearful moment as the big devil-wagon swerved from its course. The rear wheels bounded sickeningly, and for a terrible second it looked as if Old-field had found his finish. With truly superhuman effort, the muscles in his corded arms standing out like leather whips under his tanned skin, Barney straightened out the machine, jammed his foot on the pedal and sent the great white Benz howling down the stretch for the fastest mile ever run on a dirt track. A rolling volume of ap-proval from five thousand spectators matched the drum-ming beat of the cylinders as the Blitzen Benz thundered past the grandstand, with raw gasoline exploding four hundred pounds of dead engine metal into two hundred units of living horsepower."

This was dramatic reporting in an era when a speed-hungry public paid homage to its King.

9

OUTLAW DAYS

When Jim Jeffries retired as an unbeaten champion from the boxing profession in 1905 his crown had been "presented" to Marvin Hart, who was in turn knocked out by Tommy Burns, a Canadian. In late December of 1908 Burns was casually destroyed by a huge Negro, Jack Johnson, and the boxing world had a new heavyweight.

Jack London, then a newsman with the New York *Herald,* witnessed the debacle and wrote: "A golden smile tells the story and the golden smile was Johnson's . . . Jeffries must emerge from his alfalfa farm and remove that smile from Johnson's face. Jeff, it's up to you."

The new champion was unpopular from the outset, and impassioned telegrams began to pour into Jeffries' home, begging him to make a comeback "and save the honor of the white race."

Johnson readily agreed to meet Jeffries, and the match was finally arranged for the Fourth of July, at Reno, Nevada, by promoter Tex Rickard. The public loved "Big Jeff," while Johnson was condemned on many counts. Jack's numerous romances with Caucasian beauties had given rise to unsavory headlines. He was also fond of fast driving, and had collected a hatful of speeding tickets in his big Renault as he slammed recklessly through traffic. Johnson was a proud man, sure of his talents and anxious to prove his superiority in the ring.

Daily reports from Jeffries' training camp gave evidence of the ex-champion's intense desire to recapture the crown. But it was hard to overcome five years of soft living, and Jeff knew it. He was glum-faced when he climbed into the ring to face a smiling Johnson on July 4, 1910. His supporters could sense disaster in the Nevada air.

And indeed, the fight *was* disastrous. A dynamite-gloved Johnson methodically cut Big Jeff into ribbons. As one ringsider put it: "It was no prize fight—this was a massacre!"

The famous golden smile remained undimmed.

Oldfield met Jeff after the bout and accompanied the battered ex-champ on a fishing trip to Colorado. Upon their return Barney released a bitter statement to the press: "Jeff confided in me as a friend when we were alone up there in the mountains. He told me the *truth* about the fight. He told me he'd been drugged!"

Johnson laughingly denied this unfounded charge and added: "I'd be happy to beat Mr. Oldfield at his game as easy as I beat Mr. Jeffries in the ring. In fact, I've got $5,000 that says I'm a faster driver on any track."

The New York Times had revealed that Johnson "won several victories the previous winter in a southern California Racing Carnival," and that he knew how to handle himself in four-wheeled competition.

This was all Barney needed. He issued a public reply: "I note in today's paper a challenge made by Jack Johnson to race me for $5,000. . . . Automobile racing is my business and if Johnson or any other man in the world has $5,000 to bet he can beat me I am ready to meet him. . . . I will race Johnson for the same reason Jeffries fought him—for the money it will bring me."

Will Pickens was openly enthusiastic about the idea of the proposed duel and swung into action on the publicity front. Imagining fabulous gate receipts, he arranged to have the entire affair put on film for subsequent rental to theaters. He then scheduled the motor duel for late October at the Sheepshead Bay dirt track in New York.

At this point the AAA stepped in, sternly warning Oldfield and Pickens that if they persisted in this "unsanctioned farce" they would both face permanent suspension.

"They're bluffing," scoffed Pickens. "The public is behind you a hundred per cent, and the AAA wouldn't *dare* suspend us now. We're holding all the aces, so I say ignore their threat."

"I just want to get Johnson out there on the track," said Barney. "Nothing else matters."

"Fine," nodded Will. "Then we're all set."

The two sports champions met face to face on the morning of October 25, 1910. Johnson had been blasting his big Thomas Flyer around the turns in practice—and now he stripped off his heavy leather driving gloves and approached Oldfield.

"They tell me you can handle a racing car," Barney said coolly, extending his right hand.

Johnson gripped it. "I aim to *show* you I can," replied the dark giant. His fingers tightened.

The muscles on Barney's right arm swelled as he met the pressure of Johnson's grip. For a long tense moment both men exerted maximum strength. Then Jack Johnson flashed his golden smile, breaking the handshake.

"You're a strong man, Mr. Oldfield."

Barney bit off the tip of a fresh cigar. "Takes more than muscle to drive a racing car. But I guess you know all *about* racing, Mr. Johnson." He put a match to the cigar. "Or at least you will before the day is over."

The first five-mile heat was a walkaway for Oldfield in his 60-hp Knox, as the hopelessly outclassed Johnson in a more powerful 90-hp Thomas dropped farther behind with each curve.

Pickens was furious. "Listen, Barney—this has gotta look like a *race*. So slow down in the next heat and give Jack a chance to catch up. Let him pass you a coupla times. Then you can take him in the stretch."

"I'll give him what he gave Jeff—a beating he'll remember," Oldfield growled.

During the second five-miler Barney remained just a few feet ahead of the frustrated heavyweight champion, burying the Thomas in a gritty cloud of dust as he deliberately slid wide on the turns. At the finish line Johnson was helped from his car, half-blind and choking, as the film crew diligently cranked away with Pickens shouting: "Hoist Mr. Oldfield up on your shoulders, folks! That's it. Okay, Barney, wave toward the camera. Great! Just great!"

Oldfield was jubilant as he detailed the events of the afternoon for Jeffries: "And I can tell you this," he concluded. "When they took old Jack outa that car he sure *wasn't* smilin'."

True to their word, the AAA branded Oldfield an "outlaw," and placed the Speed King and his manager under immediate suspension. The ostracized pair were not even to be allowed on the grounds at a sanctioned event.

"That Johnson affair was simply a crude circus act," stated an AAA official, "and we won't stand still for this kind of farcical behavior in competition. Our decision is final and, we feel, fully justified!"

Stunned and angry, Oldfield sought a court injunction to prevent the AAA from barring his entry at the upcoming race meet in Atlanta, heatedly declaring that "my entire livelihood is jeopardized by this evil action." The attempt failed as Fred Wagner, acting under direct orders from AAA chairman Butler, refused to permit Barney to drive in Georgia.

"So who *needs* the stinking AAA?" Oldfield raged when Pickens informed him of Wagner's stand. "Plenty of people will pay to see me run on any track I pick out. Set up some fair dates, and we'll show these ginks what a circus act *really* is!"

During this early-1900s era, a county fair was often *the* big event of the year, and these elaborate three-day outings invariably attracted sizable crowds. On Friday morning a farmer would pack his wife and kids, a fresh-baked mince pie and his prize hog into the family buggy and head for the fairgrounds, for a weekend of fun and a shot at a blue ribbon. On the grounds, while the women opened picnic baskets and discussed cake recipes, the men rolled up their shirtsleeves for a brisk game of soft-ball: husbands vs. bachelors. There were potato-sack races and wrestling contests, dart games and square dancing and, almost certainly, a balloon ascension—in which a daring, bespangled aeronaut in pink tights would dizzily spin and whirl on a tiny trapeze as the great pear-shaped sac lifted itself majestically into the waiting sky.

On Saturday, the pace was stepped up, with steer roping and bronco busting. Livestock would be judged and pies carefully tasted by grave-faced mustachioed gentlemen in derby hats. A Flying Machine exhibition would cap the afternoon, and the crowd would gasp in delicious fear and delight as the intrepid pilot skimmed his flimsy airplane low over the fairgrounds, waving with one hand while he controlled his hellish contraption with the other.

Sunday was the day for the fair's star attraction, the spine-tingling automobile races, starring the one and only Speed King of the World, Barney Oldfield.

Barnstorming the county fair circuits with a racing automobile had long been an Oldfield specialty. Since 1902, and the days of 999, he had pioneered countless exhibition runs at fairs from Texas to Missouri. Many other drivers followed his example, although few of them ever matched Barney's remarkable flair for showmanship. As practiced by Oldfield, automotive barnstorming became a specialized art, with its own rules, glamour and split-second risks.

Painstaking preparation led up to an Oldfield Sunday appearance. Nothing was left to chance. Pickens was a superb advance man. He'd attend local board meetings where fair dates were allocated. Then he'd meet the fair manager and offer to furnish his spectacular automobile attraction, guaranteeing a certain number of cars and drivers led by the great Oldfield. A fee would be agreed upon. To add spice to the cake, Pickens would tell them that Barney would go for a new mile record at the fair, provided "an adequate bonus" was added to the basic appearance fee. Next, the color-splashed posters would go up. At the bars and barbershops the news would spread: "Oldfield is coming in the Blitzen!" Barney's gaudily painted railroad car would roll in several days ahead of time and be shuttled onto a siding in the manner of a circus train. All of the kids in town would head out to gawk at the silent railroad car, knowing the big white Benz was inside, waiting in the darkness to dazzle them.

Meanwhile, Pickens was at the local newspaper, handing out publicity photos and predicting a new record. He'd speak at luncheons and meetings. Then the great day arrived when Barney appeared at the station. The brass band boomed a welcome as he stepped off the train to a warm speech delivered by the mayor. Oldfield was dressed "fit to kill," and it was possible to see the mayor's reflection in the tips of Barney's shoes.

Most of the town would then accompany the Speed King to his hotel where Pickens made sure of big banners over the entrance reading: OLDFIELD SLEEPS HERE!

By Sunday afternoon, after the locally owned trotters had proven their speed in a series of tightly contested warm-up races, the dirt oval would be dampened by a ponderous horse-drawn water wagon. While this lengthy operation was underway, the Speed King would finally make his track entrance. The long, white Blitzen Benz, its polished brightwork glittering golden in the sun, would be wheeled out close to the grandstand fence, and a great cheer would burst forth as Barney climbed from the narrow cockpit to greet the crowd. After a considerable amount of fenceside conversation and light banter ("Think you can bust the record, Barney?" "Well, if I don't, I'll have to give up ten-cent see-gars!") the engine on the Benz would be started by a mechanic, with a deafening exhaust backfire. Oldfield would cant his head, listening to the sound, then slowly walk toward the long hood, his expression dark. ("She ain't runnin' right, an' old Barney knows it!" a small boy would confide.)

At the Benz, Oldfield would reach down into the vitals of the massive power plant and, within seconds, the engine would smooth to a steady idle. To the amazed farmers this was clearly a feat of magic, a touch from the master curing his faithful mount. Of course it was always a case of reconnecting a loose wire or plug lead, deliberate and as carefully staged as the exhibition itself. All part of a well-rehearsed ritual as standardized as a Barnum & Bailey trapeze act.

Will Pickens would step forward, megaphone in hand, to announce that despite a rough track and "unfavorable conditions" (these would never be specified) the fearless Oldfield would nonetheless attempt to set a new world's record "at the risk of his very life." Another lusty cheer, followed by a hushed silence as Barney grimly climbed back in the cockpit and revved the engine. Its roar was awesome.

"Are you ready, Mr. Oldfield?" Pickens would shout, drawing a pistol from his belt.

Barney would nod and pull down his goggles. The cigar in his mouth would tilt up at a defiant angle. Then, with the starting shot fired, the Speed King would blast away, wheels spinning, headed for another record.

Will Pickens made certain that the crowd was never disappointed. As "officially timed" by Pickens and a pair of hired stooges in the judge's stand, the legendary Oldfield would invariably smash the previous mark by a slim margin—to a round of fresh cheers.

The three heat races were conducted in the same flamboyant fashion. Barney owned the cars and paid the drivers. Their orders were simple: finish behind the boss. Oldfield would win the first heat in grand style. Then his star driver, Ben Kerscher "The Flying Dutchman," would usually take the second five-miler, edging out the cigar-chewing speed monarch by a car-length. Barney would look solemn and determined as the final heat got underway, and after a nerve-shattering battle with Ben—in which the lead always changed hands several times— Oldfield would rip into the final turn wheel-to-wheel with his rival, and, at the last possible moment, dive between Kerscher's machine and the fence to win by a cigar wrapper! The crowd would explode in wild acclaim. As well they should have, for, despite the "fix" of which they were unaware, they had just witnessed the greatest dirt-track exhibitionist of them all in a superb demonstration of nerve and split-second timing.

On these occasions, Barney gave his public just what they paid to see: a chilling, thrilling display of speed and daredeviltry that none would forget.

The dangers were genuine enough. Shredding tires and looming fences continually threatened, and Barney often drove to the limit, sliding the turns with the massive Benz at the ragged edge of control. Oldfield's brash comment on these calculated risks was widely reprinted: "If I go, I want it to be in the Blitzen Benz, or a faster car if they ever build one, with my foot holding the throttle wide open. I want the grandstand to be crowded and the band playing the latest rag. I want them all to say, as they file out the gate: 'Well, old Barney—he was goin' some!'"

Fred Wagner paid tribute to these spectacular county fair performances when he wrote (for *Collier's*): "Oldfield pioneered the 'circus style' of racing. At close finishes he was an artist, often managing to win by less than the width of a tire."

It is difficult to condemn such contests wholly. If the races *had* been entirely legitimate, and Barney had failed to win, the wonderous magic would have vanished. No one wants to see a Speed King lose. A host of white-haired farmers would never have been able to tell their grandchildren about the afternoon "when Barney beat 'em all, and set a spankin' new world's record right smack dab in front of my eyes!"

It was always a great day at the horse track when the fabulous Oldfield put on his show.

Barnstorming paid well—and by 1911 Barney had put aside enough money to go into private business in California. "I been promisin' Bess to retire," he said. "So, with the AAA still on my neck, I guess this is the time to keep my promise." Moross took over the Benz as well as Oldfield's two other machines: the "Giant" Knox and Darracq, while Barney opened a saloon in partnership with a former railroad conductor, Jack Kipper.

Located at 534 South Spring Street, in the heart of downtown Los Angeles, the plush establishment soon became quite popular as a "male refuge" for many stars of the sports world and the cinema. Regular patrons in-

cluded such luminaries as baseball's Frank Chance, boxing's "Kid" McCoy and Frank Gotch, the wrestler, as
well as silent screen notables Wally Reid, Dick Barthel-
mess, Lew Cody and "Fatty" Arbuckle.

A giant painting of Jim Jeffries adorned one wall, while
the "mile long" mahogany bar displayed a free lunch of
ham, turkey, cheese and pickled sausages. A quarter
would buy any two drinks in the house, and for members of the press a free beer was always on tap.

"Now you take the word 'saloon,' " said Barney to his
partner one morning after the venture was well under
way. "That word just ain't got dignity. *Bums* hang out
in a saloon. So, from here on, we call this joint the Old-
field-Kipper Tavern. Like in England, eh?"

"Barney, you got real sensitivity," nodded Kipper.
"First guy who says we run a saloon gets the boot."

However, the change failed to deter members of the
Women's Christian Temperance Union, and the good
ladies periodically marched past the site, displaying signs
which warned thirsty sinners against the evils of alcohol.

Barney found his chief source of amusement during
this period in "Mickey Finning" unsuspecting pals. He'd
offer his potential target a drink "on me," and within
moments the room would resound to the crash of a falling
body. When the dazed victim awoke and staggered to
his feet, Barney would dust him off, glare at the offend-
ing bottle and sadly remark: "Just can't buy good booze
these days. Hell, this watered-down stuff is for sissies!"

Since the AAA had declared Barney an "outlaw" he

was still not allowed on the grounds at sanctioned races, and this situation galled the stubborn showman. He got in touch with Harvey Firestone, with whom he'd been friendly since the beginning of 1908 (when Oldfield had first used Firestone tires on his Stearns), and asked for a salesman's job.

"That way they *gotta* let me into the pits," he explained. "What do you say, Harvey?"

Firestone said yes, and Barney soon began appearing at local events as a legitimate tire salesman. At each race, it seemed, he would hear about another new record set by the young, daredevil "Wild Bob" Burman.

Burman, whose nickname reflected his full-throttle driving, was not a record-breaker in Oldfield's sense of the term. It was common practice among most professionals to back off after a new mark had been set, leaving some speed in reserve for a fresh attempt on another track. Yet Burman drove wide open as long as his machine held together under him, giving no thought to subsequent performances. Therefore, in April of 1911, when Ernie Moross offered to let Burman take a shot at Oldfield's land-speed record in the Blitzen at Daytona, a startling new record was predicted.

"Oldfield told me many times about the way the old Blitzen took his sight away when he flirted with high speeds," said Burman after a few practice runs in the Benz, "but I was skeptical of this ever happening to me. Well, now I know he was right. I lost my sight out there today, and I now believe that the limit of speed is the point where it is no longer possible to see."

Despite his fear of blindness, Burman unleashed the mighty Benz for its fastest ride over the sand—and on his twenty-seventh birthday (April 23) he became the world's new Speed King, having shattered Barney's previous record by a full ten miles per hour in posting just over 141 mph for the measured mile.

Oldfield was furious at the news.

"I should never have let Ernie take over the Benz," he snapped. "He *knows* I didn't have the Blitzen wide open last year. Burman's made me look like a damn fool."

Visiting friends in Toledo later that year, Barney became so incensed to find Wild Bob breaking another of his records ("in my own back yard!") that he drove his touring car through a hole in the board fence and shot down the stretch shaking an upraised fist at the flying Burman.

Ralph De Palma was also bettering Oldfield's records with a powerful Fiat "Cyclone"—and as the 1912 competition season approached, Barney's anger and frustration mounted.

"I've gotta show those ginks I can still drive—and I don't mean on some lousy tank circuit either," he told Pickens. "Can't you *do* something with the AAA boys?"

"Their new chairman, Bill Schimph, is on our side," Pickens said. "Just sit tight and I think we'll be getting some good news soon."

At a special meeting of the AAA board, chairman Schimph was forcefully direct in his opening statement: "This organization is still growing, and we're still trying to establish ourselves as a governing power with the public. We must have their support. Now, as you all well know, there is but *one* driver in the business whose tremendous popularity is unquestioned, who represents auto racing to the public mind. We need him as much, or more, than he needs us. Gentlemen, although many of you may not approve, we're going to bring Barney Oldfield back to the AAA."

10

TO TAME A BEAST

By 1912 the American automotive industry had mushroomed, and no other industrial product could match the automobile's rate of progress. The era of mass production had begun and registrations were rapidly climbing toward the million mark. (It has been estimated that more than a thousand varieties of motor car were offered to the U. S. citizen during this robust 1900-1912 period, including such weird creations as the "Octo-auto," which utilized *eight* wheels. The inventor, M. O. Reeves, claimed that the four-wheels-in-back-four-in-front arrangement allowed the car "to travel easily over a road full of chuckholes.")

Vigorous track competition between marques was responsible for almost daily improvements in the average passenger vehicle, and when Ray Harroun won the first 500-mile classic at Indianapolis in 1911 in a Marmon

"Wasp," a rear-view mirror (used on the Marmon) soon became standard equipment on non-racing cars.

Cadillacs were being sold with electric self-starters. Improved frames, brakes, clutches, springs, transmissions and ignition systems all resulted from rugged track meets, hill climbs and endurance contests.

Several giants had risen in the ranks since Oldfield's layoff. Among them: AAA's 1911 champion, amiable Ralph Mulford, a former Baptist Sunday school teacher, who always competed in a high starched linen collar and necktie; handsome David Bruce-Brown, a wealthy Yale student who astounded the racing world by climbing into a Fiat and defeating an all-star international field at Savannah in 1911; "Terrible Teddy" Tetzlaff, a quiet Westerner whose intense desire to win brutally asserted itself on the track, making him one of the sport's most feared (and sometimes hated) competitors—and, just emerging from obscurity, a small 120-pound Californian named Earl Cooper, with the calculating mind of a mathematician, who would become the greatest of them all.

The season's big opener was the 300-mile Santa Monica Free-For-All in May, with Tetzlaff, Bruce-Brown, Cooper and Caleb Bragg set to dispute the victory. When the AAA announced Oldfield's reinstatement late that April, Barney immediately entered the lists, declaring he would win the California event behind the wheel of a Fiat.

On May 4, while the nation's newspapers headlined the tragic death toll of the ill-fated *Titanic*, Oldfield pulled a wool cap over his head, donned a cloth face mask (to combat dust), and prepared to resume his career. He realized that a triumph here would put him back on top, and was out to prove that a year's absence had not affected his nerve or skill.

At the 25-mile point in the race it was Tetzlaff, Bragg and Oldfield, with Bruce-Brown in for fresh casings. Pushing the Fiat to its limit, Barney took over second in the following lap, only to suffer a 30-minute forced stop caused by a broken spring bolt. Resuming the battle, he turned lap after lap as fast as the leaders until a thrown tire on the back stretch cost him another 13 minutes. Hopelessly out of contention, he refused to accept defeat. Maintaining a furious pace, he was now averaging almost 90 mph around the twisting road course. Finally his front axle snapped, sending the big red machine into a ditch; for Oldfield, the race was over, but his gallant drive had demonstrated that he was still a championship contender.

The second annual 500-mile race at the Indianapolis Speedway took place on Decoration Day. Barney attended as a spectator, since Carl Fisher refused to honor his entry. ("Maybe the AAA can forget all the rules he broke, but I can't. Oldfield will never set another tire on these bricks.") This 1912 "500" was a heartbreaker for Ralph De Palma, who led brilliantly in his Mercedes until piston trouble forced him out just five miles short of the checker. He gamely pushed the heavy car back to the pits as Joe Dawson's National swept by to a $25,000 victory.

While Oldfield was in Indianapolis he encountered one of his ex-rivals, designer-driver J. Walter Christie, and an important conversation ensued.

"I've got my front-drive up for sale," said Christie. "She's stored away in Long Island. You could have her for a song."

"That car's a beast, Walt, and you damn well know it," replied Oldfield.

"That's why I'm only asking a thousand," Christie agreed. "*You* could handle her, Barney. You've tamed more than your share of stubborn iron on the dirt."

Oldfield pursed his lips. Then he squinted at Christie. "Make it $750 and you got yourself a sale."

More than one driver had come to grief in a front-drive Christie since the first of the freakish track creations rolled from Christie's shop on the Hudson River waterfront in 1904. During the Vanderbilt Cup Race, in '05, George Robertson sheared both front wheels in a ditch. Two years later, at Pittsburgh, Christie himself suddenly lost control of a newer model in a turn and broke a leg and arm as the car rolled viciously. Other drivers had attempted to hold down the fishtailing machine at speed and failed. The last of the infamous front-drives was completed in 1909, and this was the car Oldfield purchased for $750 in the late spring of 1912.

The Christie's engine (rated at a fantastic 300 hp) was tilted back, allowing the front of the racer to be covered with a ventilated hood, creating a crudely streamlined effect. Lacking a clutch, the Christie had to be push-started, and since it was quick to overheat it was only suitable for short sprints. But it was frighteningly fast, and after trial runs Oldfield stated: "This is positively the quickest two-mile car in the world today."

In order to cash in on this dramatic pronouncement, Will Pickens lost no time in letting it be known that his star attraction was once more available for a summer of barnstorming. Printed circulars, mailed to county fair secretaries, read in part:

BARNEY OLDFIELD IS BACK AGAIN!

More daring, more chance-taking than ever! Age cannot wither this remarkable man, the most sensational professional athlete the world has ever known. "Speed Kings" come and "Speed Kings" go but the REAL Speed King goes on forever.

Suppose old John L. Sullivan could fight faster and more furiously today than when he was in his prime. Where could they house the crowd he would draw? . . . Since his reinstatement by the automobile association the greatest, the most sensational racing daredevil in the history of this most hazardous of all sports is now a bigger crowd-drawer than ever before! Select the day you usually have the poorest attendance—and let BARNEY OLDFIELD turn it into the BIG day at your fair.

Don't wait to write—WIRE the moment you get this circular. Barney will send along his terms in a personally-written letter which will tell you how to get the dollars and cents benefit of his services. WIRE NOW!

In addition to Christie's fire-breathing man-killer, Old-field had acquired a Cino and a "Prince Henry" Benz to complete his racing stable. With his drivers, Lou Heinemann and "Wild Bill" Fritsch, he began a profitable three-month tour of the Northwest. Mammoth 24-sheet posters on thousands of board fences heralded Oldfield's efforts to tame the "Killer" Christie (on which Barney had painted the legend: FIRESTONE TIRES ARE MY ONLY LIFE INSURANCE).

Over track after track Barney fought the powerful nose-heavy machine around the turns as the crowd gasped. Oldfield learned to handle the car at faster and faster speeds.

"If there's a Hell for auto racers," he said after one of these runs, "it ought to consist of driving Walter Christie's speed monstrosity around a mile track!"

However, by mid-September, in Cleveland, Oldfield wrestled the treacherous front-drive to a new two-mile record (officially approved by the AAA) of 1:35.8.

Indeed, the Christie had finally been tamed.

In early October, fresh from his tour of the county fairs, Oldfield attended the Vanderbilt Cup Race in Milwaukee as an observer. De Palma captured this event with a Mercedes and was expected to repeat his triumph at the accompanying Grand Prize event scheduled for October 5 over the same rain-rutted 7.8-mile road course.

Practicing for the Grand Prize in a Fiat, David Bruce-Brown left the circuit as a result of a blown tire. The popular young star died in the accident—and his slightly

damaged machine was offered to Oldfield as a last-min-
ute replacement.

"There'll be no time for you to learn the course," he
was warned by the Fiat's owner, E. E. Hewlett. "Are
you game?"

"Gas 'er up," Barney ordered. "But don't expect me to
win."

Oldfield didn't win; he took fourth at the end of the
409-mile grind. Caleb Bragg emerged the victor after a
race-long duel with De Palma. Making a desperate bid
to pass on the last lap, the Italian struck the rear of
Bragg's machine and rolled his Mercedes over a barbed-
wire fence into a cornfield. Impaled on the tough corn
stalks, De Palma's abdomen was slashed and both of his
legs were broken, but he survived—to be declared AAA
Champion for 1912 at the season's close.

Before the year ended, Barney had invaded a new
domain, the world of the corner nickelodeon.

Hollywood's Mack Sennett, who was a racing fan (as
well as the creator of the Sennett Bathing Beauties and
the Keystone Cops), approached Oldfield that winter at
the veteran's Spring Street saloon.

"Barney, did you ever think of getting into the flicks?"

"An' have some dame throw a custard pie in my face?
No, thanks!"

"But you'd play a *hero*," Sennett told him. "You could
save Mabel Normand from a black-hearted villain by
outrunning the Express. I even have a great title: *Barney
Oldfield's Race For A Life*. Whattya say?"

"Mack, have a beer on the house—you just hired your-self a new movie star!"

In this lurid Sennett-produced melodrama a fiendish Ford Sterling chains the distraught Miss Normand to the railroad tracks, leaving her to a most dreadful fate. Barney, informed of her plight, jumps into his touring car and grimly sets out after the Los Angeles Express. Averaging a mile a minute, he overtakes the train and reaches the frantic girl just in time to pull her from the path of the onrushing locomotive. The villain is dispatched and Oldfield is warmly embraced for his heroic drive.

After seeing himself in action on the screen, Oldfield sadly shook his head: "For this kinda actin' I *should* have been hit by a custard pie!"

The 1913 season began at Playa del Rey, where Barney's Christie won over Tetzlaff's Fiat by less than a second in a furious sprint race on the banked boards. Teddy's riding mechanic, George Hill, was impressed with Oldfield's performance and told him so in the pits.

"Why not come to work for me?" Barney offered. "I happen to need a mechanician, and I've heard good things about you."

"But Tetzlaff pays me twenty-five bucks a week and fifteen per cent of the prize money," Hill declared. "That's a good setup."

"I'll give you *fifty* a week—and *twenty-five* per cent of what we win. Deal?"

They shook hands on it.

In this pioneer period of two-man cars, the "mechanician"—or riding mechanic—served a very vital role, hand-pumping to maintain gas and oil pressure at appropriate moments during the race and keeping a close lookout on cars approaching from behind. He was also necessary in frequent on-the-track tire changes and mechanical adjustments. Actually, these men often performed amazing feats in order to keep their cars in the running. During the Long Island Stock Car Derby, in 1909, Louis Disbrow's steering was seriously affected when a pin dropped out of a front rod. His mechanic climbed out onto the long hood. There, with his feet braced, hanging to the radiator cap with one gloved hand, he reached down and held the steering rod together as Disbrow drove the remainder of the rough 20-mile circuit. A good riding mechanic, therefore, was worth his weight in gold—and Oldfield was willing to gamble on a man such as Hill.

"The Imperial Valley road race is comin' up next month," said Barney. "I want you to take my Fiat down there and learn the course. Got things to do here in L. A. and I may be late getting away. So *you* do the practicing."

It was an odd arrangement. Each day Hill would receive a telegram from Oldfield with the message: "Keep Practicing!" The course was extremely difficult, ranging through Brawley, Holtville, Calexico, El Centro and Imperial over rutted dirt roads spanned by eight-foot irrigation ditches, four to a mile. (The competing cars were forced to leap them in steeplechase fashion.) For a week before the event itself Hill pounded over these roads with the Fiat. On the final day, February 22, with the race set for a pre-noon start, Barney stepped off the train.

"How's the course?" he asked.

"A nightmare," replied Hill. "Without practice it's impossible."

"That's what I sent *you* down for, George. You can tell me all I need to know."

Hill sighed, and they climbed aboard the Fiat.

Nine competitors got off the line at four-minute intervals—with Barney's Fiat the last car away at 11:57. Frank Verbeck's Napier failed soon after the start with magneto trouble, while Tetzlaff held the lead out of Brawley, only to crash at Holtville as his car struck the railroad tracks. Oldfield had instructed Hill to rap him sharply on the back when it was time to shift down for a blind curve, and by Calexico he had passed all six cars to lead the contest. Favorite Ed Lyons, the previous year's winner, overturned his National in an effort to close on the Fiat, as Barney, at 70 mph, sailed over the irrigation ditches. (At times the wheels of his car would not touch the ground for 50 feet.) With thousands of farmers cheering him on as rain turned the dirt to gumbo, Oldfield gunned over the finish line to capture a $3,200 first-place prize, having covered the 203 miles in four hours, 41 minutes.

"It was just like I figured," grinned Barney to his

astonished riding mechanic. "You told me all I needed to know."

That night they celebrated in Mexicali.

A month later, at Owensmouth, California, Tetzlaff won the main, with Barney chasing him all the way. The Sunday edition of the Los Angeles *Times* breathlessly chronicled a "near-miss" when a small R. C. H. pulled onto the course directly into Oldfield's path. Columnist Bert Smith described the action: "It seemed beyond human ability to avert an awful collision . . . yet Oldfield hurled his great racer toward the embankment and missed the little R. C. H. by an inch. The giant Fiat crashed over the embankment as the rear wheels slewed around to an angle of 45 degrees. It was here that Oldfield demonstrated the rare ability that has won him so many racing laurels. He shot wide of the track and over the ploughed land . . . and righting his machine in a great cloud of debris he ripped back onto the course and, amid the defiant blasts of his Fiat, disappeared down the narrow boulevard . . ." This spectacular incident may well have cost Barney the race, since he finished less than 12 minutes behind Tetzlaff's larger Fiat.

In late April, at Bakersfield, Oldfield blitzed the sun-red Christie around the mile oval fast enough (in 46.4) to lower the world records of Burman and De Palma by more than a full second. One report described the machine "reeling like a drunken sot, with its naked exhaust emitting clouds of fire . . . while frantically excited women waved hankies and parasols."

Barney was satisfied. He had been angry and frustrated when De Palma and Burman smashed his speed marks in 1911; now he was able to reverse the pattern and regain his record-holding stature. The Christie proved an excellent substitute for the Blitzen Benz.

The season was a full one. Over the Fourth of July weekend, with Hill beside him ("the best man I ever had at my right"), Oldfield entered the rugged 444-mile Los Angeles-to-Sacramento Road Race, and was leading at the halfway point near Fresno when a wrong turn led him five miles off course. A broken drive chain delayed him further, but he managed to finish in the money for third, with only 18 cars surviving in the 50-car starting field.

"We began this one at midnight," he later recalled, "and kept warm by sipping from a bottle of Napoleon Brandy which I had George wrap up special for us so it wouldn't break. Without that bottle I guess we just might of froze solid behind the wheel!"

While Barney was in Sacramento, Earl Cooper won the main at Tacoma, Washington, with the car he would make famous: his white No. 8 Stutz. Cooper was destined for his first AAA Championship that year, and Earl's next stop was the Santa Monica Road Race, held in early August over an eight-mile macadam course near the ocean.

Oldfield had joined the Mercer team for this contest,

and sped off to a first-lap lead at the flag, with Tetzlaff steaming up behind him. On the third lap, however, Cooper hammered past Tetzlaff to dispute the lead with Barney—and an unrelenting two-man battle was under way. Tire changes sent them both to the pits, and by lap 20 Cooper had established a four-minute advantage. Within seven laps, however, Oldfield had regained two-and-a-half minutes. Earl kept his foot down and maintained the lead until, with but two laps remaining, the Stutz began to slow as it neared the pits. Cooper bumped in on a flat. His mechanic struggled to remove the wheel as Earl anxiously waited to resume the battle. As Oldfield came roaring past, the Stutz driver vaulted from the cockpit, pushed his mechanic aside, and yanked the wheel off, hurriedly replacing it with a spare. He had less than two laps to catch the flying Mercer.

A careless burst of exuberance cost Oldfield the prize. Seeing Cooper in the pits, he gunned into the Palisades turn at far too great a speed. In the resulting slide across the rough macadam both rear tires exploded. Cooper's Stutz blasted by the crippled Mercer to take the flag with a decisive six-minute margin.

"Earl has won the day," declared Oldfield as he wiped the sweat from his face in the pits, "but there will be *other* days. And now, if you'll pardon me, gents, I will get myself outside a couple of cold beers!"

11

COURAGE AT CORONA

The unique and picturesque "circle city" of Corona some fifty miles southeast of Los Angeles, in the foothills of the Santa Ana mountain range, was the site of the season's next major West Coast event. The only city in the United States based upon a perfect circle, the small community was divided neatly into four quarters. Completely encircling it was newly paved Grand Boulevard, 70 feet from curb to curb and originally built as a giant three-mile horse track over which "gentlemen riders" could race and exercise their blooded steeds. However, with the emergence of the motor car, Grand Boulevard had been paved, and now formed a natural speedway. Since the town was ripe for expansion due to its favorable location in the citrus belt, several wealthy citizens banded together to form the Corona Auto Club for the purpose of publicizing their community with an annual auto race. Backed by the AAA, this initial 1913 event was awarded national status, which automatically guaranteed vast crowds and a choice field of drivers. It was expected that Oldfield and Cooper would repeat their blistering Santa Monica duel here at Corona. After a tour around the smooth thoroughfare Barney predicted lap speeds in excess of 90 miles per hour.

"A wide-open throttle and plenty of nerve will win the day," he stated.

Earl Cooper had other ideas. Tire trouble had almost cost him victory at Santa Monica and he planned new tactics for Corona. Arriving for practice a full week before the contest he drove the course at varying speeds, in an attempt to solve the problem of excessive tire wear. After countless trips around the big circle he determined that he could win with an average speed of approximately 75 mph. This would guarantee a minimum of pit stops. He would let his competition set the hot, tire-destroying pace.

On the evening prior to the race, in the ballroom of the Glenwood Mission Inn (while thousands of motorists huddled outside near campfires on roads near the course) the five top favorites—Oldfield, Cooper, Tetzlaff, De Palma and Spencer Wishart—were surrounded by admirers. Barney, sporting an ivory-headed cane, a large diamond ring glittering from his little finger, vowed he would win the upcoming battle on the basis of sheer speed. "That Mercer of mine is full of go," he said, "and I'm gonna ask her for all she'll give me."

"What about tires?" asked Cooper.

"My pit's full of 'em," replied Oldfield. "Tell you what, Earl—*you* worry about tires."

Cooper nodded. "I intend to," he said quietly.

Race day, September 9, was warm as over 100,000 spectators lined the three miles of Grand Boulevard, a hundred deep beyond the curbs. Special trains (some from as far as San Francisco) had brought a mass of enthusiasts to witness what promised to be a great event. The city was arrayed in bright colors. Banners flew; flowered booths sold food and souvenirs, and the local brass band sent out festive music.

"Beautifully gowned ladies of high rank," smugly observed the press, "rode back and forth in their great machines, as they admired our little city."

An all-star field lined up on a wide boulevard, shaded by rows of palm and pepper trees, for the two-in-one main event. (The medium car class, for engines up to 450 cubic inches, would run with the unlimited class.) Behind a pace car, the field was flagged away to strident cheers, and Barney's big yellow No. 1 Mercer immediately slammed into the lead just ahead of Tetzlaff's Fiat and Felix Magone in a Stutz.

The pace set by Oldfield was brutally fast—and within a few miles tires began to burst against the sun-scorched pavement. Cooper, playing a waiting game, lapped at a steady, conservative 75, while Oldfield was clocked, during one tour, at 98. As the leaders pitted, Cooper placed his white Stutz into the lead on lap 14, but Barney had

135

repassed him by lap 22, only to pit for fresh rubber and give the front-running position to Magone.

By lap 49 Magone had dropped out, along with Tetzlaff, De Palma and Wishart—all victims of the savage pace set by Oldfield. Barney, now plainly in command once more, was forced to ease off, due to a roughening surface; the "ideal" track was beginning to break up. Oil spots had appeared and the cars were forced to the outer edge of the pavement. On lap 45, his tires again in ribbons, Oldfield roared into his pit, furious as Cooper motored serenely into the lead.

"Hurry up with those damn wheels," Barney shouted to his perspiring crew. "We've got a race to win!"

Accelerating wildly back into the fray, a fresh cigar between his teeth, Oldfield set out after the Stutz and re-passed Cooper within three trips around the big circle. Since the other serious competitors were now all out of contention it was a repeat of Santa Monica: Oldfield vs. Cooper. But as the race ground on, Earl was running a full two laps to the Mercer's rear. Even with his numerous pit stops Oldfield's average was some three miles per hour faster, and it appeared that he would avenge his Santa Monica loss.

Then—disaster!

A nine-year-old boy on the fringe of the crowd could no longer contain his mounting excitement. He darted between his father's legs and ran out onto the boulevard to urge Barney on. As Oldfield rounded the turn on lap 60, with his bellowing Mercer at full throttle, he saw the boy directly in his path. A shocked gasp arose from the crowd as the charging machine bore down at better than 90. Without hesitation, using all of his strength, Barney courageously swung the big car hard left, in a skidding, tire-screaming arc. He missed the boy, but forfeited control. Under the violent sideways thrust a front wheel buckled and the Mercer launched itself, a huge yellow projectile, into the trees and foliage.

A spectator was felled with a broken leg, and Barney's riding mechanic, Frank Sandhoffer, was scalped after being pitched from the cockpit. Miraculously, Oldfield himself escaped without serious injury. He stumbled from the smashed racer.

"Did I miss him?" he asked desperately. "Is the kid okay?"

"He's fine, Mr. Oldfield," a track official assured him as Barney slumped dizzily to the ground. "Thanks to you, he's just fine."

Earl Cooper motored on to win Corona—and the 1913 AAA crown.

12

FROM BEACHEY TO THE VANDERBILT CUP

The year 1914 was memorable not only for the outbreak of war in Europe, but also for the release of D. W. Griffith's mammoth Hollywood masterwork, *Birth of a Nation*, the emergence of a talented new rookie with the Baltimore Orioles, George Herman ("Babe") Ruth, and the serialization of Miss Pearl White's cliff-hanging antics in *The Perils of Pauline*.

Also very much in the news were the fantastic cross-country duels between Barney Oldfield and Lincoln Beachey.

THE DEMON OF THE SKY

vs.

THE DAREDEVIL OF THE EARTH

for

THE CHAMPIONSHIP OF THE UNIVERSE!

Thus did Will Pickens announce, via scores of gaudy 24-sheets, this hair-raising series of exhibition races, which elicited an overwhelming response from a thrill-seeking public.

Pickens had branched out; he no longer confined his talents to publicizing automotive contests. By 1914 he had promoted almost every type of colorful money-making spectator sport—from bicycling to balloon racing—and was now managing twenty-six-year-old Lincoln Beachey, who had gained great fame as the nation's "Master Birdman."

As with motoring, aviation was still in its pioneering stage, and although much progress had been made since the Wright brothers sent their ponderous Flying Machine soaring over the hills at Kitty Hawk in 1903, the airplane was still a dangerous, unpredictable invention. Beachey, who had been a balloonist since he was fifteen, made his initial flight in a plane (after Glenn Curtiss had given him free instructions) in 1910—and soon became America's most daring stunt pilot. Linc's heart-stopping exploits included flying under bridges, hedge-hopping freights (by letting his tires tap the roof of every third car) and picking up dainty lace handkerchiefs with a hook fastened to the wingtip of his Curtiss biplane. He defied the might of Niagara Falls by plunging into the spray-fogged gorge and emerging unscathed on the far side—and had even flown *inside* a building (San Francisco's Machinery Hall during the Panama Pacific Exposition). His hazardous specialities were the Dive of Death, the Reverse Spiral and the Ocean Roll, all of which Beachey devised and perfected for his many exhibition appearances.

"Give me enough power and I'll fly a barn door upside down," he once said, and his Curtiss was only slightly more airworthy.

A four-cylinder, 40-hp pusher type, with a wing-span of 28 feet, its tail and wings were simply cloth stretched over wood and hooked to the body by bamboo poles. Beachey sat, exposed to the elements, on a small bicycle seat, pushing the wheel backward or forward to move the elevators, or turning it to right or left to manipulate the rudder. The engine was located at his back, above his shoulders, while he perched at the extreme front end of the plane, stabilizing the weird craft by leaning to either side as it tipped crazily off-balance. (The whole affair was designed to be quickly dismantled so that it could be shipped, in four packing crates, from town to town.)

A man of somber moods, who walked with a limp as a testament to numerous crashes, Beachey refused to conform even in his chosen profession. He eschewed the usual leather helmet, cavalry pants, puttees and ornate boots worn by most stunt fliers. Instead, he flew in dark pin-striped business suits, and his trademark was his large checked English golfing cap which he always reversed with a flourish just before take-off. He hated crowds, and would deliberately swoop down on a row of open bleachers, forcing the spectators to "hit the planks." (This bitterness stemmed from the fact that he had seen the body of more than one luckless pilot stripped and his craft shredded for souvenirs after a fatal crash. "I like to scare 'em so they scatter like chickens in a barnyard," he declared.)

Some three dozen stunters had been killed trying to emulate his daring, to "pull a Beachey," and the moody Sky King retained a clipping of each tragedy, inwardly blaming himself for these deaths. He had retired in 1913 because of this guilt, but was lured back to aviation when a Frenchman, Adolph Pegoud, achieved a vertical loop in the skies of Europe. Beachey promised he would become the first American flier to duplicate this feat in the United States and he not only kept this promise but made the trick one of his main specialties, looping up to 80 times in a single afternoon. He always insisted on $500 for the first loop, and $200 for each succeeding one—cash in advance.

When Pickens got the idea of combining the extraordinary talents of his two star performers, Oldfield and Beachey agreed with Will on a three-way profit split—and before the 1914 season ended they netted over $250,000. Crowds packed in to see Barney wager his track skill against Beachey's air savvy. In one town the Christie (or the Fiat) would triumph; in the next it would be the Curtiss, and the local press accounts of these carefully staged "battles" were characteristically lurid: "Oldfield's auto seemed like a frightened rabbit scurrying away from the big bird of prey directly above it. At times there seemed scarcely more than a few inches of clear sky between the fearless motorist's head and the wheels of the plane."

Actually, these two-way duels were almost as dangerous as they looked. At the Los Angeles Ascot track, Beachey's crankcase exploded, demolishing the engine and causing the prop to saw its way through control wires and connecting struts. The Curtiss dropped like a hurled stone into a grove of walnut trees as Beachey landed unhurt in a patch of freshly turned earth. On another occasion, Beachey swept ahead of Barney on the straightaway, skimming down directly in front of the charging Fiat to take the checker. The propwash all but blew the cigar from Oldfield's mouth. Suddenly the plane's engine quit cold, and Beachey's Curtiss nosedived into the dirt as Barney whipped his car into a slide in order to avoid a two-way crash. The aviator was hospitalized for a few days, but was soon back in the sky.

Sometimes the Oldfield-Beachey combination proved equally dangerous *off* the tracks. At Milwaukee, late that summer, Barney insisted on visiting a lady friend who worked in a dance hall.

Beachey, who hated adverse publicity, pulled at his wool cap and hesitated.

"Maybe you'd better go alone," he said. "I might be recognized."

"In this joint they wouldn't recognize the king of Sweden," Barney assured him. "This I guarantee!"

However, Oldfield had forgotten the piano player—a chunky six-footer who immediately greeted Barney by name as they arrived. He then turned to Beachey.

"Ain't you the famous sky-boy?" he demanded.

Beachey nodded.

"Then, let's see if you can *fly!*" And with this he picked up the small aviator and held him high above his head. "Now, go on fella, spread yer wings."

Barney had seen enough. He pulled Beachey from the big man's grasp as easily as a toy is removed from a shelf. Then he drew back his right fist and drove it into the beefy face of the piano player. The force of this blow sent the fellow rocking back on his heels, across the dance floor and through the closed swing doors. He fell flat on his back in the street.

"You killed him!" exclaimed Beachey in horror. "My god, Barney—he's *dead!*"

Oldfield leaned down and listened to a steady heartbeat. "Naw," he said, "he just learned a fact." Barney grinned broadly. "When an aviator flies he has *got* to have a aeroplane."

Always wise in the ways of publicity, Will Pickens seldom missed a bet where free newspaper space was involved—and when Barney casually remarked that "with a little practice I might be able to handle a crate like the Curtiss" this was all the stimulus Pickens needed. He added a few touches of his own and released a statement to the press: "Oldfield Will Loop the Loop." Pickens quoted his star: "I have been making a few flights with the idea of getting into the flying game on a professional basis. I know I can give my loyal public plenty of thrills when I get to looping."

Beachey read the piece in high glee at the pits between races while Oldfield looked embarrassed.

"If you want to start looping right now just let me know," said the airman. "I'll be happy to lend you my plane. How about it, Barney?"

Oldfield never took him up on the offer—and within a few short months aviation's "brave young warrior" was gone from the skies.

Lincoln Beachey had plunged to his death in San Francisco Bay.

The chain of events leading up to the classic Oldfield–De Palma clash for the 1914 Vanderbilt Cup began the previous year when the Mercer factory hired the popular Italian to captain their official racing team. Under his supervision, three new Mercers were constructed: a pair of very powerful 450-cubic-inch models and a smaller 300-cubic-inch machine. De Palma personally took over one of the larger cars, modifying it to his own satisfaction, while Caleb Bragg piloted the second 450-incher. In the course of the 1913 season Bragg was replaced by Spencer Wishart, a spirited competitor in the manner of Burman and Oldfield, who generally drove (as one pressman noted) "at bolt-loosening, rod-breaking speeds." Eddie Pullen was brought in to complete the team.

De Palma won the 100-miler at Brighton Beach that year for Mercer, and carefully prepared his car for the big Vanderbilt Cup contest, coming up in February. He had won the Vanderbilt in 1912, and after posting a straightaway mark of 117 mph in the big Mercer Ralph felt that he could repeat the victory in 1914.

The Mercer company representative, Finley R. Porter,

knowing that the two hottest names in the sport were De Palma and Oldfield, couldn't resist the chance to have both of these giants in the Mercer stable. Without consulting De Palma he set up a deal with Barney, and proudly announced that Oldfield would henceforth drive for the factory.

Informed of this, De Palma angrily resigned from the team after a heated comment on the "gross unfairness" of Porter's action. His fast, much-modified Mercer was therefore taken over by a delighted Oldfield, while Wishart and Pullen remained in command of the other two machines. Barney saw a chance to achieve his cherished ambition; this year he would win the great Vanderbilt Cup Race.

A trial run in the car convinced him of its potential. He was more optimistic than usual as reporters surrounded him after the test.

"This one's a real dandy," he said, patting the Mercer's hood.

"De Palma's after another car," a pressman needled. "He says he's going to see you eat his dust."

"Listen, son," said Barney, "if that spaghetti-pusher shows up—which I doubt—I'll run circles around him. And if there's any dust to be eaten, he'll do all the swallowing!"

The Oldfield–De Palma feud was again choice news.

With the big race only a month away, De Palma became desperate. He had no car to pit against the hot Mercer, yet he was determined to win the cup over his confident rival. Then Ralph thought of the old "Gray Ghost" Mercedes with which he had won the Vanderbilt as well as the Elgin Cup in 1912. The machine belonged to a close friend, E. J. Schroeder, a millionaire New Jersey lamp manufacturer, and had been "put out to pasture" after De Palma had smashed up the German car in the 1912 Milwaukee Grand Prize contest. Ralph got in touch with Schroeder and got his okay to ship the battered Mercedes to the West Coast. In less than three weeks De Palma had rebuilt the Ghost—and though the Mercedes could not match Oldfield's Mercer on top speed it could knife through the corners fast enough to remain solidly in contention.

While the papers played up the two-way "grudge battle," a crack 15-car field was gathering: Oldfield, Wishart and Pullen for Mercer, Cooper and Gil Anderson for Stutz, Verbeck and Dave Lewis for Fiat, Billy Carlson for Mason, Guy Ball for Marmon, plus five other lesser entries representing Isotta, Sunbeam, Apperson, Alco and Touraine—and De Palma with the lone Mercedes.

Santa Monica had been chosen as the site for the 1914 Vanderbilt by the new AAA chairman, Richard Kennerdell, bringing the race to the West for the first time. (The eight previous Cup events had been held in Long Island, Savannah and Milwaukee.)

"Granting to Southern California the privilege of running the W. K. Vanderbilt race is the highest honor ever paid the Pacific Coast by New York City," declared Leon T. Shettler, head of the racing committee. "It is also the best advertisement California has had since ex-Mayor Alexander wore knee-pants."

The long 8.4-mile road course, lined with palm and eucalyptus trees, offered man and machine a genuine challenge. It began off Ocean Avenue, heading into the sharp right-angle turn at Wilshire—called Death Curve— down an engine-straining three-mile straightaway to the Soldier's Home Curve, through Brentwood Park, along the rolling foothills to Ocean Park, then down to the San Vicente Boulevard turn which led back to Ocean Avenue.

Will Pickens provided a typically dramatic full-page ad for his star in the glossy Vanderbilt Program booklet: "Barney Oldfield's driving is the result of thorough experience, great strength and superhuman nerve, coupled with a coolness that leaves him more collected in the face of imminent danger than the average man would be at pink tea . . . Knowledge and skill, and not recklessness, are the dominant factors in Oldfield's driving. Luck plays a very small part in his performances. His wonderful ability to think quickly and act with unerring precision have gotten him out of many a tight corner which would have spelled disaster to many a less efficient driver."

This same booklet listed among the entries one Baron von Richenbacher in a Mason entered by Hollywood's Mack Sennett. As it evolved, the Baron did not drive in the Vanderbilt, but was nevertheless kept under close scrutiny by several gullible track officials as a possible German agent working for the Kaiser. (Germany was poised on the brink of the First World War, and all German aliens were regarded with suspicion in the States.) The mysterious "Baron" was, of course, Edward Vernon Rickenbacker who had been active in auto racing for four years—and who was soon to become America's greatest air ace. His entry as Von Richenbacher had been devised as a gag "to liven up the program," and no one was more amused than Eddie himself.

Friday, February 13, was set as the first practice day— with three of the superstitious drivers staying off the course. Wishart turned the best lap time with his Mercer in just over seven minutes, but the mark was bettered the following afternoon by Oldfield at six minutes flat. Wishart reduced this to 5:58. Speeds were increasing.

Death struck on the 17th. Dave Lewis broke the steering knuckle on his Fiat at Old Soldier's Curve, and a spectator died in the crash. De Palma finally made an appearance with the gray Mercedes, but in his warm-up lap he burned out a bearing on the long straight.

"If he gets that old boat fixed I'll run him clear off the course," laughed Barney, reducing his official time to 5:59.

"Beating that cigar-chewer," replied Ralph, "will be easier than eating two plates of spaghetti."

The weather abruptly ended practice as three days of rain drenched the roads, and Oldfield was bedded with a nagging head cold. Sympathetic fans overflowed the lobby of his hotel, each offering a "surefire" home remedy for the ailing speed idol. By February 23, Barney was back at the wheel.

The De Palma Mercedes burned another bearing and was towed back to the garage—causing Oldfield to assert that his rival was no longer of any concern to him. But De Palma wasn't quitting. Two days later he was back on the road, having put his trust in a new product, Kelly's Metal, which the local inventor guaranteed against heat. If a single bearing made of this special metal burned out, Mr. Kelly promised to refund the $200 De Palma had paid for the job.

"I don't want the $200," Ralph assured him. "I want to collect the $3,000 first prize and beat Oldfield in the bargain."

The Gray Ghost's best lap was a slow 6:37, some 38 full seconds behind the Mercer's time, but De Palma was content to have made the grid. He had a plan in mind which had nothing to do with top speed.

On February 26, as the 15 cars lined up to do battle (Lewis was back from the hospital in a Mason), more than 125,000 impatient fans lined the course. After almost two weeks of practice and rainstorms they were primed for action, and the grandstand gave Oldfield a substantial cheer as he slid into the cockpit of the Mercer. The applause for De Palma was equally unrestrained. Under a clear sky, starter Fred Wagner flagged away the first car, Grant in his Isotta. Wishart's Mercer was next, 15 seconds later, followed by Anderson, Pullen, Lewis and Oldfield (with George Hill beside him as riding mechanic). De Palma's Mercedes was 11th off the line—and what one writer termed "the gas duel of the century" was at last underway.

Set for 35 laps, the race was immediately led by Wishart, with Oldfield riding fourth. However, by the second lap, Wishart's engine turned sour and he nursed his car into the pits, giving the front spot to Pullen in the smaller 300-inch Mercer. Gil Anderson paced Oldfield for second—with De Palma running far back in the field.

On the seventh tour Barney turned into the pits in order to have a spare wheel lashed to the big Mercer, and was instead offered a fresh box of Corona Queens by his confused crew chief. Oldfield's reply scalded the air, and the wheel was quickly put aboard. De Palma had worked his way smoothly into fifth when Barney's Mercer roared from the pits.

Number 13 proved unlucky for Eddie Pullen, for on that lap he slid wide in a turn and rammed a wooden barrier, demolishing the right side of his car. Anderson's Stutz inherited the lead, as Oldfield brought in the only remaining Mercer for rubber, gas and oil.

"Has De Palma pitted yet?" he asked.

"Nope," said Barney's crew chief. "In fact, what with everybody makin' all these stops, he's riding second right now behind Anderson."

"Then get me the hell *out* of here!"

Oldfield savagely resumed the fight, slewing wildly around the turns as he angrily attempted to overtake the Mercedes. By lap 19, with Anderson out due to a broken crankshaft, De Palma calmly led the field. Within two more laps Barney had gunned the Mercer into second, just over a minute behind the Gray Ghost. Lap 24 found the two rivals separated by only eight seconds, and the next tour saw Oldfield blast by on the long straight, kicking fountains of dust and gravel into the air. A broad smile indicated his state of mind.

Only 10 laps remained and the spectators were shouting themselves hoarse while the seesaw battle raged on. De Palma would close fast as Oldfield threw the ponderous Mercer around the turns in a pillar of dust, but the Mercedes was left behind on the straights where high speed paid off.

The vital question was: how long could De Palma continue? His tires still seemed in fair condition but surely his gas and oil would not last the entire 35 laps. Oldfield need only concern himself with tires, since his full-throttle bursts punished them severely—but he could not afford another pit stop, despite the fact that his left front casing was beginning to shred.

De Palma sliced by on the inside as Barney eased off to save rubber, but the Ghost led the Mercer by less than a car-length as they entered the pit straight. In the hope that Oldfield would assume he was in trouble, De Palma signaled his crew that he'd be in on the next round, making sure that Barney saw the gesture. He then allowed the Mercer to pull ahead.

It is impossible to say whether or not Oldfield was taken in by this ruse, because at that instant his badly shredded tire let go and he was forced into making a final pit stop.* De Palma, who had planned from the

---

* Many accounts of this race misstate the facts as sworn to by Oldfield's riding mechanic, George Hill. "They say we pitted for a new tire to be on the safe side, figuring De Palma was also going to stop. Well, that's just not true. The tire blew on the road and Barney *had* to come in for the change."

outset to go the full distance, motored past with a wave as Barney's crew fought to replace the wheel. It took them 70 agonizing seconds.

Back on course, with only four laps remaining, Oldfield drove like a man possessed, gaining some 11 seconds on each trip around the circuit, but time was running out; the handicap was too severe. De Palma whipped past the checker a bare 200 yards ahead of Barney's charging Mercer to win the ninth Vanderbilt Cup.

The Italian's drive had been a splendid one, and the Los Angeles *Times* gave him full credit: "De Palma, knowing the speeds of the two cars, had figured out his gas consumption to the last drop, paced his speed just fast enough to win, and thus saved himself from making a pit stop for fuel, tires or oil. It was a great victory."

Only five cars, all far behind the leaders, completed the 294-mile event. Billy Carlson was third in a Mason, Cooper fourth in his No. 8 Stutz and G. Joerimann was fifth with a Touraine.

As predicted, it had most certainly been "a duel between titans."

13

ON THE BRICKS AT INDIANAPOLIS

A foreign invasion of the Indianapolis Speedway had been launched in 1913, when a $20,000 first prize lured some of Europe's premier drivers across the water for a run on the bricks. The French Peugeot team, headed by wine-swigging Jules Goux, had been invincible on European soil during 1912, winning every race they entered, and the factory sent Goux and another of their aces, Paul Zucarrelli, to the third running of the 500-miler. England, Italy and Germany were also represented, and the United States assembled its best cars and drivers to stem the foreign tide. America's main hopes rested with the two rival marques, Mercer and Stutz.

The clownish Goux, fortified in the pits during the long contest by six bubbling bottles of imported French champagne, had run away with the race, nosing out

Wishart's Mercer and the Stutz of Charlie Merz to win at an average speed of just under 76 mph.

The Peugeot developed into a remarkable machine. In an era of monsters (as typified by the 14-liter Fiats) it drew amazing performance from a small, fast-turning engine machined to very close tolerances. Built like a precision watch, the Peugeot's engine was responsible for writing finis to the theory of speed by brute power.

In 1914, however, the most exciting car in America was the Stutz "Bearcat," a rakish two-seater that snared the heart of every grandfather and gay blade in the nation. The brainchild of Harry C. Stutz (who had fielded the first racing car to bear his name at Indianapolis in 1911), the agile Bearcat was only one of several extremely successful models produced by this gifted designer. So popular was the Bearcat, that by May of that year it was not possible to buy a new model anywhere in America. Demand had outstripped supply.

That same month saw Barney Oldfield switch from Mercer to Stutz, a move that put him behind the wheel of a new four-cylinder 434-cubic-inch team car for the fourth annual running of the Speedway Classic at Indianapolis. In accepting Barney's entry, Carl Fisher remarked: "I once swore Oldfield would never drive the '500,' but he seems to have mellowed a good bit since the days when he defied every rule in the AAA book so I will no longer stand in his way."

First-prize money had soared to $39,750 in 1914, and again drew the cream of Europe. Eight foreign stars appeared, spearheaded by another strong French team—

and once more the U. S. met them with a crack contingent of men and machines: Oldfield, Cooper, and Anderson for Stutz; Bragg and Wishart for Mercer; Tetzlaff and Carlson for Maxwell; and Rickenbacker and Haupt for Duesenberg. Other top Americans (some in foreign cars) included Burman, De Palma, Mulford, Grant—and Joe Dawson, the 1912 Speedway winner.

But Peugeot's Jules Goux (teamed with Georges Boillot) seemed confident of a second French victory. "We will have to go a little faster this year perhaps, but we will take your fine money. We only worry about each other." (He was referring to the French Delage team of René Thomas and Albert Guyot and to the swift Excelsior in the hands of Joseph Christiaens.)

Arthur Duray's independently entered "Baby" Peugeot was the center of much discussion. When the Parisian made up his mind to compete at Indianapolis he was casting about for a suitable mount when he encountered Jacques Meunier, son of the wealthy Chocolate King, at a boulevard stop. When Meunier heard that Duray needed a car he quickly solved the problem: "Take mine!"

This Peugeot was not a racing model; it was a sports runabout, and proved to be the smallest car at Indianapolis. Its 183-cubic-inch motor was dwarfed by such giants as the 445-inch Maxwell, and pre-race estimates gave it little chance against the large-bore machines. (Even the Delage boasted a 380-inch piston displacement.) Yet this Baby could step, and Duray would prove it.

A crowd of 100,000 surged into the Brickyard to fill the stands to capacity on race day, May 30, and a new 500-mile record was in the air. Disappointingly, Ralph De Palma was a nonstarter with his newly imported Mercedes since he had been unable to cure a serious chassis vibration which rendered the car too dangerous to drive on the rough brick surface. The fastest qualifier was Georges Boillot in his factory Peugeot, beating out Goux with a shattering 1:30.17. Teddy Tetzlaff registered 1:31.7 with the Maxwell, completing the top trio.

Nattily uniformed in his white cloth helmet and white coveralls with STUTZ lettered across his chest, Oldfield tried vainly to elicit high lap speeds from his new machine. After three frustratingly slow runs he was allowed a fourth official try, and managed to qualify 29th among the 30 starters, barely making the field. (In all, 40 cars had tried for the grid.)

Promptly at 10 A.M. the competitors moved smoothly away in eight rows behind the pace car for a rolling start. The flag snapped down and the pacemaker pulled to the apron, releasing the tightly bunched pack in a blue-gray cloud of exhaust. Choked by Castor fumes and burning rubber, Oldfield deliberately dropped back to allow the air to clear. Riding in 25th place at the end of the first lap around the 2.5-mile brick saucer, he gradually began picking off the tail-enders. Jules Goux forged to the front on the fifth lap, but soon pitted with a flat, giving the prime position to Caleb Bragg. Lap 10 saw the Excelsior leading Boillot's Peugeot but within three tours René Thomas took over for an extended pace run.

On lap 16, fighting to move the Stutz into contention, Oldfield had worked his way up to 19th place ahead of such aces as Mulford, Burman, Cooper, Rickenbacker and Tetzlaff—but he had already been lapped by the leaders. Chassagne shot out of control on the next lap and overturned his Sunbeam on the northwest corner, luckily sustaining only slight injury. Still pushing, Barney was 12th at the 60-mile mark, then gained another place on lap 32. Tetzlaff's Maxwell had caught fire and retired.

On lap 44, at 110 miles, a crash occurred which removed one of the top Americans, Joe Dawson. Journalist J. E. Schipper gives this precise account of the accident: "Dawson, riding in seventh, was following Gilhooley's Isotta when the latter blew a right rear shoe while near the outside of the track. The Isotta struck the cement wall at the outside and then started across the course to the inside, turning over twice and landing on the driver and mechanic in the middle of the bricks. There was a narrow space between the wrecked Isotta and the cement wall. Wilcox, driving the Gray Fox, was close behind and got through this space. Back of him came Joe Dawson, but just as Dawson approached, the Isotta mechanician began to crawl from the wreck toward the outside wall. Dawson realized that to follow the Gray Fox would be to strike the wounded mechanic. Instead, he veered to the inside of the wreck, but his Marmon skidded, turned turtle and landed on the grounds. Dawson was severely injured internally and was removed to the hospital."

The first Stutz to retire was Anderson's—due to a loose cylinder bolt—and he was ordered to wait in the pits as relief for Oldfield at the 100-lap point. Barney, meanwhile, was still creeping up, having edged into the top ten by lap 48. Rickenbacker rode his tailpipe with the Duesenberg, and Cooper followed with the third Stutz.

Lap 62 provided a surprise, as Duray in the Baby Peugeot led the field. He continued in this position for five more laps, until a tire change sent him into the pits. Obviously, speed did not depend entirely on cubic inches.

Oldfield continued his steady assault as Burman and Wilcox called it quits. Lap 64 saw Barney riding in eighth; and by lap 72, with two more cars out, he was seventh, ahead of Bragg. (At this point, Albert Guyot headed the pack in his blue Delage.)

Gil Anderson climbed into the Number 3 Stutz as Barney pitted for tires midway in the contest. At this 250-mile juncture the field had been reduced by more than a third, and Thomas led in his Delage, hard pressed by Boillot.

By lap 120 Cooper's relief driver left the course when a tire exploded, breaking two wheels, and Bragg's crankshaft had forced his retirement. Anderson was now holding sixth ahead of Christiaens' Excelsior. (The Wishart Mercer also fell victim to crankshaft trouble.)

Lap 147 spelled the end of a gallant effort by Boillot. He was leading when a tire exploded in the second turn. The casing whipped from the wheel, striking the Frenchman's arm and ripping off his necktie. Although he reached the pits without aid and resumed the race after a new wheel had been fitted on the Peugeot, he was forced out shortly thereafter. (The impact of the blow-out had broken the Peugeot's frame.)

Oldfield was back in the cockpit by lap 150, holding off Christiaens' Excelsior for fifth, and the vast crowd had now pinned their dimming hopes on the veteran. With 50 laps to the flag, four French cars led the lone Stutz, and Barney represented the last serious American threat. Yet he could not extract enough power from his car to improve his position. He had come from last place to fifth in a machine which was hopelessly outclassed in speed—and unless mechanical ills sidelined the four leaders (Thomas, Duray, Guyot and Goux) he could only hope to maintain his hold. The drumming, rhythmic purr of the foreign machines contrasted sharply with the rough bark of the Stutz as the final miles rolled away, and the cars finished the race in that order: Delage, Peugeot, Delage, Peugeot and Stutz. (The winning speed for Thomas was a new record: 82.47 mph.)

Sadly, but with evident pride, *The Automobile* summed up the results: "Today has been a bad day for America. Our hopes have been crushed to earth one after another, and when 300 miles of the distance were covered those on whom we had staked most were gone—but thanks to the veteran track driver, the hero-worshipped Barney Oldfield, we got fifth place honors, the Stutz being the only American car to land in the first seven, averaging 78.15 miles per hour (fast enough to have won the previous year's event) . . . A thunder of cheers burst out from every throat when Barney Oldfield brought the first American car across the line."

Only 13 competitors received the checker. The Stutz had split the foreign ranks by holding off Christiaens' Excelsior, which took sixth two laps behind Oldfield. Filling out the top ten finishers: Harry Grant, Sunbeam; Charles Keene, Beaver Bullet; Billy Carlson, Maxwell; and Eddie Rickenbacker, Duesenberg.

The fourth annual 500 was over, a singular triumph for France, but America had not lost without honor.

On July 4, with the European outbreak of World War I less than a month away, Oldfield and Gil Anderson appeared on the newly completed two-mile oval at Sioux City, Iowa, to represent Harry Stutz again. A 300-mile main event, to be run over what was termed "the finest dirt track speedway in the nation," offered a purse of $25,000 and was hotly contested from the outset. Eddie Rickenbacker in a Duesenberg scored the outright victory over Spencer Wishart's Mercer—and Anderson was fourth for Stutz. Barney had dropped out early with engine trouble.

In late August, while newspapers headlined the conflict in Europe, the Stutz team made another unsuccessful try at the famed Elgin Road Races in Illinois. In the Chicago Auto Club Trophy, Ralph De Palma took the checker first in his new German Mercedes, and Stutz had to be content with Anderson's second over-all. Barney was fourth.

The following day, in the Elgin National Trophy, Oldfield managed a third for the marque, but again De Palma had proven unbeatable (with Eddie Pullen in for

Late in 1910, after being placed on suspension by the AAA, Oldfield turned to a circus style of barnstorming. Here he is about to overhaul one of his own hired drivers in a carefully staged last-lap victory.

Helms Hall

Seated behind the wheel of his road-equipped Benz, Oldfield poses with
a pal, baseball's immortal Ty Cobb.

In 1911, still under the cloud of his AAA suspension, Barney tackled the saloon business, opening a plush establishment on Spring Street in Los Angeles. This "mile-long" bar, with its free lunch, became a hangout for the sports crowd. Here a friendly reporter could always be sure of a drink on the house. Boxer Jim Jeffries was a frequent visitor.

Helms Hall

It wasn't often that Oldfield would consent to pose with his bitter track rival Ralph De Palma, yet the two were brought together for this photo by middleman Earl Cooper, a great driver in that wild era.

Helms Hall

Back in racing after his layoff, Oldfield purchased the "Killer" Christie, and set out to regain his position as the nation's number one daredevil by taming the treacherous front-drive. Note the Firestone slogan.

Helms Hall

In 1914, under the canny promotion of Will Pickens, Barney engaged the fearless young stunt-flier, Lincoln Beachey, in a series of incredibly hazardous duels: Plane vs. Auto for the Championship of the Universe! Here, in this gag shot arranged by Pickens, Beachey applies a match to Barney's giant cheroot.

Helms Hall

Begrimed and content after a national AAA victory at Venice, California, in March of 1915, Oldfield still retains the tattered stub of his cigar.

Helms Hall

In mid-1917 the revolutionary all-enclosed Golden Sub made its debut. Designed and built by Harry Miller, whose specials would later dominate Indianapolis, the car almost became Oldfield's coffin in a flaming crash that year at Springfield. Note Barney's ever-present lucky kerchief and the diamond ring he sported on the little finger of his right hand.

Detroit News

January of 1918 found the Sub's confining aluminum top stripped away, and in this lightened, safer version Oldfield won his match race that afternoon at the Ascot track against Louis Chevrolet's Frontenac.

Helms Hall

Having retired from competition after 25 years of speed, Barney became a "business tycoon" when Harvey Firestone backed a special tire, the "Oldfield," in 1919. As company president, the veteran stands before a dealer's window displaying shots of 999 and the Miller Sub.

BARNEY OLDFIELD
IN PACE MAKER

OFFIC
SPEEDWAY
1139
COBURN→

Always a popular favorite at Indianapolis, Barney drove the pace car there in the 1920 running of the 500-mile classic. Note the famous "Oldfield underhand grip" on the wheel.

Russ Catlin

Another "all-star" group of drivers. Left to right: Tommy Milton, Jimmy Murphy (winner of the 1921 French Grand Prix), Benny Hill, Eddie Hearne and Oldfield.

Russ Catlin

A grimly determined Oldfield poses with Harry Miller in May of 1932. The miniature racer represented plans for a 300 mph record run which was then in the planning stage. Despite the advancing years, Barney claimed he could win back the land-speed record for America (then held by England's Sir Malcolm Campbell).

Helms Hall

To prove his stamina, Oldfield drove an Allis-Chalmers faster than any tractor had ever been driven, at Dallas, Texas, in October of 1933. He had notched up another world's record.

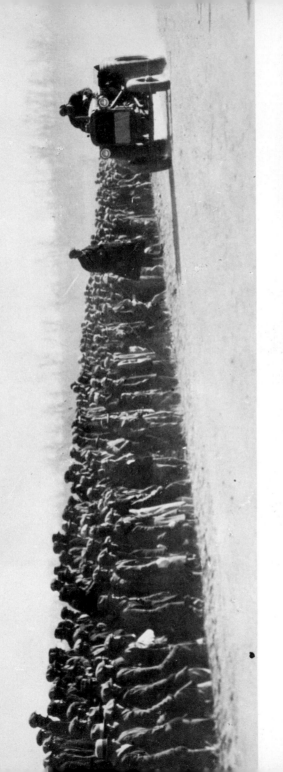

During the '33-'34 period, Barney slated a series of exhibition runs with farm tractors. He felt that this was one way he could keep his name before the public. In this photo excited farmers line a dirt road to watch the veteran thunder past.

Helms Hall

In constant demand as a starter for countless events in the thirties, Oldfield energetically flags down the winner at a California speed meet.

Gar Wood, speedboat champion, Harvey Firestone, Henry Ford and Oldfield pose for a photo which marks the end of an era.

Helms Hall

One of the last shots ever taken of Barney Oldfield. The veteran flashes
his familiar grin at Detroit's Automotive Golden Jubilee in May of 1946.
He was officially honored as one of America's great pioneers at the Jubilee
banquet. (In October of that same year, at 68, he died at his home in
Beverly Hills, California.)

Helms Hall

second). In this tragic race Spencer Wishart's hard-pressed luck finally ran out. On lap 15, at full throttle, he had attempted to pass Otto Henning on a narrow section of road and sideswiped the Henning machine. As Wishart fought for control, swerving to avoid a line of horrified spectators, his Mercer plunged from the course into a tree. A fractured skull and internal injuries claimed his life.

14

A FABULOUS DRIVE IN
THE CACTUS DERBY

The death of Spencer Wishart, coupled with his own inability to win a victory for Stutz, exerted a depressing effect on Oldfield during October of 1914. More than one sports writer had broadly hinted that "the grand old man of auto racing" was slowing down, that he should have retired when he was on top of the game.

Barney's depression turned to anger, however, when an acid-penned columnist stated: "Oldfield should stay with the hippodrome circuit, where he belongs. On a tank town oval, with his own paid stooges behind him, he might still be able to give the hicks a thrill or two. In open competition, he's a washout."

"Look at this drivel," Oldfield roared, thrusting the sports section at Bess. "This fat-headed jerk says I'm a washout. I think I'll go right down there to the office and break his big nose for him!"

Bess put aside the paper and smiled indulgently. She had weathered many a stormy display of Oldfieldian temper, and now she looked up at Barney, shaking her head.

"No, dear, that won't do you any good. Remember the time in Mexico, when they threw you in that awful Tijuana jail and took away all your clothes? It would have been much better if you'd simply *not* broken that newspaperman's big nose."

"He called me a bum," protested Oldfield. "Nobody calls me a bum. Not even Woodrow Wilson could call me a bum!"

"Let's hope he never does. I should dislike to see the President with a broken nose."

Oldfield's scowl was replaced with a grin. "Darn you, Bess, you never take me serious."

"But I do, I really do," she said. "It's just that there are other nonviolent ways to prove a point. For example, instead of raging at these columnists, why not show them they're wrong? Enter the Stutz in the Cactus Derby next month and win it. That would set them *all* back on their ears."

"Hell, that's a stock car grind," Barney said. "No racing machine has ever won it. In last year's Derby I didn't get much farther than San Diego, and that Simplex I drove was a tough wagon."

"But you set the *record* to San Diego."

"And broke the car doing it. No, the Stutz just wouldn't last out the Derby."

"It lasted 500 miles at Indianapolis," Bess said.

"Sure—and 500 miles on a brick oval is a lot different from almost 700 miles of potholes and sage. I talked to Cooper about the race and he said we'd be plain fools to try it."

"You were a plain fool when I married you," smiled Bess. "Now let's stop all this gab. Tell Harry Stutz to announce your entry. Show 'em the old warhorse can still gallop!"

"Do you *really* think I could do it, Bess?"

"Not unless you do."

"All right, then!" Oldfield slapped the table with his fist. "I'll show all of 'em. I'll run a race they'll never forget. And I'll win, too!"

Bess quietly took Barney's hand. "Of *course* you will," she said softly.

Automotive historians have named the Cactus Derby as the roughest road race ever held annually in the United States. Prior to 1914, six of these back-breaking, car-busting mountain and desert marathons had been run from California to Arizona—and merely finishing was considered a laudable accomplishment, since the tortuous terrain beyond Los Angeles reduced the heavy, stripped-down stock machines to crumpled junkpiles before they could reach the finish line at the Territorial Fairgrounds in Phoenix.

The first Derby was held in 1908, instituted by the Auto Club of Southern California as part of a vigorous campaign for better roads. (Since no roads whatever existed throughout most of the race route the basic idea was sound.) Only four entries summoned up enough nerve to set out across the 480 miles of wilderness that year, and two of them became lost in the Colorado desert, allowing Col. F. C. Fenner (in a White Steamer) to record an unchallenged win at an average speed of 17.6 mph.

By 1909 more than a dozen cars defied the odds, but cracked frames, burst radiators, bent axles, fractured fuel lines and broken steering knuckles were the order of the day. Eight battered machines staggered into Phoenix, with Louis Nikrent posting a win for Buick.

The Derby's third running saw a Kisselkar garner the laurels, with its driver, Harvey Herrick, also winning the fourth event in 1911. During this race (in which the distance was increased by 100 miles—dipping below the border into the barbarous countryside of the bandit, Zapata, in Northern Mexico) the irrepressible Teddy Tetzlaff blasted his crimson Fiat into the lead, only to wrap the big Italian car around a telephone pole near La Mesa.

Ralph Hamlin brought his Franklin in ahead of the field for the 1912 affair, despite a series of blinding flash floods—and Olin Davis, in a Locomobile, attained the victory in 1913. (Oldfield had competed in his first Derby in '13 with a borrowed Simplex, with which he led into San Diego. A broken drive shaft finished his run at Yuma.)

In addition to the usual first-place money (in this case, a modest $2,500), a special medal would be awarded to the 1914 victor. The idea had come about when automotive editors Al Waddell of the *Times,* Willard Wood of the *Herald* and Charles Branaman of the *Examiner* were chosen as official pathfinders. After they had laid out the arduous new 671-mile route (with Nikrent as chauffeur in his Paige), Wood proclaimed: "It'll sure take a master driver to win this one!" To which Branaman added: "I'd stack the Derby up against any race in the world."

Waddell nodded. "You boys have given me a thought. Let's present the winner with a bronze medal as 'Master Driver of the World.' We could have the words inscribed right on it, in a diamond setting. It'd be great publicity."

Thus the seventh running of the Cactus Derby offered a unique title to accompany the cash prize, and many of the country's best rough-road competitors accepted the challenge.

Two previous winners were on hand for this 1914 race: Olin Davis and Louis Nikrent. Other strong contenders were Derby veteran Bill Bramlett, Cliff Durant (millionaire son of Chevrolet's dynamic president, W. C. Durant), Ted Baudet, Billy Carlson and Louis Chevrolet himself. After a teeth-jarring practice run over the new route Chevrolet declared: "This is the hardest event ever undertaken by a racing automobile."

A dozen other entries swelled the field, with Oldfield's track Stutz completing the line-up.

"Those wire wheels of Barney's will collapse before we're out of the mountains," Nikrent predicted. "He'd be better off leaving that kiddy car of his safe at home!"

George Hill, again riding with Oldfield, also expressed doubt. "What Nikrent said makes sense," he told Barney. "Maybe we ought to try and carry a full set of spares."

"Two's the limit," Oldfield stated. "That larger gas tank is enough extra weight to worry about. We'll just have to take our chances and hope the wheels hold up."

By the morning of November 9, as the 20 machines assembled at Eastlake Park in Los Angeles, a cold predawn rain had soaked the roads, an omen of the bad weather ahead. The Derby was a three-day battle, taking the cars over El Cajon Pass, north toward Victorville and Barstow, east to the first overnight stop at Needles, across the Colorado River, north once more to Kingman and Peach Springs, then east through Seligman to Ashfork, angling south to Prescott, the second night's stop, then on into Phoenix. En route the cars would face wind, choking alkali dust, desert sand, silt, mud, jagged rocks, narrow, boulder-strewn gullies—and the bridgeless obstacle of New River. A trainload of racing officials and pleasure-bent Los Angeles businessmen were set to follow the contest in their "Howdy Special," meeting the cars at each night control and urging them on from various points along the route which paralleled the tracks. (Oldfield had wisely installed a personal masseur on the Special, anticipating the severe muscle strain engendered by the rugged terrain.)

Ted Baudet was flagged away at 5:25 A.M. and the massive rear wheels of his Paige threw up fantails of spray as he gunned for Needles, 301 miles to the east.

Separated by two-minute intervals, Durant was sent off next in his modified Chevrolet, followed by the Reverend Earl Schnack in a Ford and Olin Davis in his fast Simplex. Oldfield was fifth off the mark in the same white Stutz he had driven at Indianapolis.

The rain-slick pavements out of Los Angeles accounted for the first two casualties (both cars had skidded into telephone poles), and as the cars left the flooded boulevards and essayed the steep climb through Cajon Pass, the overstrained engine on Anderson's Kisselkar forced his retirement. Schnack's Ford had paced the field into San Bernardino, but Oldfield had managed to edge by on the narrow summit of the pass to gain an early lead.

As the competitors dropped down into the desert a Metz pulled to the side of the road with a broken front axle, its racing already done. The sky cleared between Victorville and Barstow, and Durant's Special moved up to engage Barney's Stutz; Olin Davis closed with the leaders to make it a three-way sand duel.

With the first overnight control still not in sight two more cars suffered breakdowns: Schnack's Ford retired with a broken universal, and a DeDietrich shattered its axle east of Barstow. Half a dozen machines were now out of the running.

Barney had managed to open up a slight gap on Durant and Davis when a sudden backfire ignited the intake manifold. Smoke began boiling up from the engine compartment.

"We're on fire!" shouted Oldfield, skidding the Stutz

to a halt. "Grab the extinguisher, George. I'll get the hood open."

With Barney clawing at the hood straps, Hill attempted to free the fire extinguisher from its bracket on the cockpit wall, slashing his right hand in the process.

"Quick—or she'll blow up on us!"

Hill sprayed out the flames and the hood was slammed down as Cliff Durant racketed past, happily shouting "Get a horse!" Oldfield put the Stutz in gear and accelerated into immediate pursuit.

"That cut looks bad," Barney observed. He pulled a kerchief from his coat pocket. "Use this. Stop the blood, anyhow."

"I'll see the doctor in Needles," promised Hill, knotting the cloth around his injured hand. "Think you can catch Durant?"

"Just *watch* me!"

Oldfield not only repassed the Chevrolet Special but held off a spirited bid by Olin Davis, rolling into Needles with a six-minute advantage over Durant. Louis Chevrolet was the fourth man in, with Nikrent fifth. The cars were then placed in a guarded corral, upholding the rule that all repairs must be done on the road.

That evening, while most of the town celebrated the arrival of the Derby, Barney lay stretched out in a hotel bed, with the masseur working diligently on his neck and shoulder muscles.

"Tonight I feel just like what they call me," he groaned.

"And what might that be, sir?"

" 'The Grand Old Man of Racing.' And I mean *old*."

Hill entered the room, his hand freshly bandaged.

"What'd the doc say?" asked Barney.

"Infection's set in. I've got to have it taken care of again when we hit Prescott."

"So now I've got me a one-handed mechanic."

"We'll make out," said Hill. He winked at the masseur. "Damn if you don't look in worse shape than I do!"

Oldfield grunted. "I *am!*"

At daybreak, under a clouded sky, the surviving cars were flagged away for Prescott, a 236-mile dash over impossibly rough country. Oldfield had gotten off to a poor start due to a balky radiator cap which refused to turn, but the Stutz sounded healthy, with a solid bite to the exhaust, and Barney was confident that he could make up the delay.

Beyond Needles, the course led to the Colorado River, where a pair of heavy planks had been laid across the railroad trestle, enabling the cars to bypass the ferry and cross under their own power. Speeding to hold a slim lead, Cliff Durant dived onto the trestle, but missed the planking. He bumped across, wheels thumping against the ties; upon reaching the other bank he discovered that a spike had pierced one of his casings. It cost him six minutes to make the tire change. (Olin Davis took over the race, with Baudet's Paige close behind.)

Oldfield was gaining rapidly on the leaders when trouble struck again. On the mountain grade, out of the small mining town of Gold Road some 30 miles from Needles, the Stutz began to misfire on the steep ascent. Abruptly the engine died.

"How about a push?" shouted Barney as a group of husky miners moved toward them. "She's not geared for a climb like this."

The big car was muscled to the top of the grade, and the engine restarted on the downhill run.

Furious at the minor delays which had hounded him, Barney opened the throttle wide over the next 50 miles, overhauling Baudet on the approach into Kingman. Now only Davis was ahead of him.

"Rock!" warned Hill, but the warning came too late.

The jagged stone stabbed deeply into a rear tire, but Oldfield refused to stop.

"We've lost *enough* damn time," he snarled. "With your bad hand we'd be all day getting that wheel off. We'll ride into town on the rim and make the switch there. I need gas anyhow."

Beside the Howdy Special in Kingman, Oldfield hastily installed a new wheel with the train's passengers shouting encouragement from the windows. "Atta boy, Barney! You can do it!"

The slashed tire dropped Oldfield to fifth—and he roared out of Kingman into a fierce hailstorm eight minutes behind Olin Davis. His first-day's lead seemed irretrievably lost.

However, near Peach Springs, the Stutz slammed past a surprised Nikrent to move up a notch.

"Now let's hope some of our bad luck rubs off on

Davis and the boys," said Barney. " 'Bout time for a switch."

This was precisely what happened. Olin Davis was squatting by his Simplex, wrestling with a tire when Oldfield ripped by. Carlson's Maxwell (which had been closing on Louis Chevrolet) was the next casualty. Forced to walk into the nearby town of Stringman to replace a broken wheel, he returned to discover that bandits had adroitly stripped the Maxwell—with the carburetor, magneto and other three wheels all missing! Billy Carlson was out.

Miserable weather continued to harass the contestants. Between Seligman and Ashfork the hail turned to sheets of icy, driving sleet, and it was at this point that Louis Chevrolet's car came to a final stop. A well-meaning sheepherder, making an effort to assist Chevrolet in Seligman, had poured several gallons of water into Louis's gas tank in the mistaken belief that the big cans contained fuel. Six miles beyond the small Arizona town Chevrolet's machine spluttered to a standstill. As the frustrated driver worked desperately on the engine Cliff Durant appeared, bumping along slowly on a broken wheel. An exchange was quickly made: one of Chevrolet's wheels was put on Durant's car and Louis climbed up to ride as mechanic.

Barney now dominated the race once again, sweeping into the second night control at Prescott with a substantial 48 minutes over the Davis Simplex.

That night he sent a telegram to Bess:

HAD TOUGH RUN TODAY THROUGH RAIN AND
HAIL. STUCK ON MOUNTAIN AT GOLD ROAD. LOST
TIME, BUT OVERTOOK EVERYONE. HAVE A GOOD
LEAD IF ONLY I HAVE LUCK TOMORROW. MUCH
LOVE, BARNEY.

"How's the mitt?" asked Oldfield as Hill returned to
their hotel.

"Better," George replied. "Afraid it won't be much use
in an emergency though."

"We've *had* our full share of emergencies," declared
Barney. "From here on I figure you'll just need to hang
on tight into Phoenix."

On November 11, the final morning of the Derby, 11
cars were flagged away for the 134-mile run to the fairgrounds. Weather reports listed two rain-swollen rivers
between Prescott and Phoenix, while the 7,000-foot climb
into the mountains and the descent to Skull Valley would
be tricky business with the storm still raging. Barney
knew that all of his road skill would be required to maintain his hard-won advantage.

In attempting to catch the flying Stutz, and at the same
time fend off the rush of Nikrent who again posed a
serious threat, Olin Davis plowed into a mud bank,
breaking a drive chain and totally disabling his Simplex.
His long run was over and Louis Nikrent now became
Oldfield's chief pursuer.

Bill Bramlett's Cadillac had also left the course, diving
off a 12-foot embankment just beyond Prescott. Though

the car had barrel-rolled it had fortunately landed back on its four wheels and was found to be roadable. Shaken, but determined, Bramlett resumed the chase.

Safely out of the mountains, Barney was guiding his car over the slippery roads with caution, knowing that another ruined tire would allow Nikrent's Paige to overwhelm them. The miles unreeled behind the rolling wheels of the Stutz, and the fairgrounds at Phoenix seemed, at last, a solidly attainable destination.

"How far?" Oldfield asked, his face blue with cold as he drove, head lowered against the biting wind.

"About 20 miles more," replied Hill. "Then we're in the money!"

Barney's return grin quickly faded when they rounded the next curve to face the foaming waters of New River.

Oldfield and Hill exchanged a look of despair, then Barney slid from the seat, stripped off his coat and wrapped it over the hood. He then drove the Stutz slowly along the bank until they reached what appeared to be a fairly shallow section.

"Hang on," he warned Hill, "we're going across."

The big car seemed to hesitate for a split second, then dipped forward into the swirling river. For a time, Barney urged on the machine as a jockey urges on his mount, and their passage was steady. However, nearing the halfway point, the engine sputtered once . . . twice . . . then fell silent. It would not restart.

"The flywheel has swamped her," said Hill. "I was afraid we wouldn't have enough clearance."

"Can't we push?"

"I'm no damned good with this hand," George replied, "and you can't move over three thousand pounds of automobile by yourself."

"Well, I've sure gotta try!"

Although the Kincaid Special had pulled out with a twisted axle and the last Metz entry had overturned, Nikrent's Paige was going strong. Bramlett's stubborn Cadillac was only a few miles behind—with Ted Baudet and the Durant/Chevrolet car still very much in the running. Every minute Oldfield spent at New River brought his competitors closer.

Barney's efforts to move the car were useless. All four wheels of the Stutz were firmly mired in the river mud. The two men suddenly fell silent, listening. A distant buzz—increasing to a steady roar; the sound of an engine.

"Nikrent!" groaned Barney.

Helplessly, Oldfield watched the Paige motor serenely cross the river and disappear on the far side.

"Did you see that satisfied look on his face?" asked Hill. "He's got this race in his hip pocket now and he knows it. Why, in our shape, it'd take a miracle to—"

"There's our miracle," Oldfield cut in, pointing across the water. "A mule team!"

Before the two animals could be hitched to the Stutz, however, Bill Bramlett's Cadillac navigated the river without a misfire.

"See you in Phoenix—if you ever get there!" shouted Bramlett.

"There goes second place," said Hill.

"The hell with second place," snapped Barney. "We can still *win* this damned race. Now, c'mon, whip up these mules and let's get moving."

Slowly the heavy Stutz was sucked free of the clinging silt. As the two laboring mules pulled it over the top of the bank Oldfield dropped the gear lever into second and let in the clutch. The motor exploded to life, the chain snapped—and the two thoroughly frightened animals bolted into the sagebrush with the muleskinner charging after them.

"The way they're goin' they'll beat Nikrent into the fairgrounds!" laughed Hill, as Barney ripped the hood open. Hurriedly he cleaned the plugs and carburetor, then vaulted back to his place beside Oldfield.

"How much time did we lose in that lousy mudhole?" asked Barney.

"Fifteen . . . twenty minutes at the outside."

"Then we've got a fighting chance. We can't beat Nikrent in, but we *can* take him on elapsed time if this buggy holds together!"

The final miles to the finish were taken as fast as the Stutz could cover them, with massed crowds on both sides of the road shouting Barney on as he crouched over the wheel, intent on extracting the last ounce of power from the laboring engine.

Bill Bramlett in the Cadillac was having his own troubles. In heedless pursuit of Nikrent he had skidded in a patch of sand in the outskirts of Phoenix, demolishing a fence. The steering was put out of commission, but the engine was still firing. More determined than ever to reach the flag, Bramlett and his mechanic had torn two long posts from the splintered fence and fastened them to the axle on the inside of each front wheel. Then, with each of them holding a post so that the car did not wander off the road, they painstakingly guided the damaged Cadillac toward the fairgrounds.

Nikrent had crossed the finish line, but could not yet claim the victory in elapsed time since the Stutz was still coming, the mud-spattered vehicle sliding wildly on the wet roadway as Barney kept the throttle open.

Incredibly, Oldfield's bad luck had not yet ended . . .

"Look out!" shouted Hill.

A wooden crosswalk loomed directly ahead. The Stutz struck the heavy planking and became airborne, the hub of the left rear wheel gouging a long sliver from a stout telephone pole. The car half spun, then slammed to earth.

"How much farther?" shouted Barney.

"Just a mile or two," Hill told him. "We're almost in!"

The band was playing as the laboring Stutz, its motor coughing erratically, entered the fairgrounds' mile dirt oval and circled the track, jolting to a final halt in front of the main grandstand.

As the crowd thundered his name, Oldfield wearily removed the clot of mud which had once been a cigar from the side of his mouth, pushed up his goggles and slapped Hill on the back. "Well, what about it, George? Did we win?"

"I can give you the answer to that one," said Louis

Nikrent, reaching up to shake Barney's hand. "You sure did, you old bastard—and I don't mind saying there's no man alive I'd rather have beat me!"

Oldfield had covered the 671.4 miles in 23 hours, for an average of just over 29 mph, besting Nikrent by 36 minutes in over-all time. Ted Baudet was third, Durant and Chevrolet fourth and Bramlett fifth. Only two other cars were credited with finishing.

Among the many telegrams of congratulation handed Oldfield at the Adams Hotel that evening was one from Bess. It read:

> PLEASE SAVE BOOZE PARTY TILL YOU GET HOME
> AND I WILL HAVE ONE WITH YOU. AM SO HAPPY
> THAT YOU WON. BEST LOVE AND KISSES.

Later that night, in the hotel's lavishly decorated banquet hall, George Purdy Bullard, Attorney General of Arizona, presented Barney with the bronze, diamond-studded medal of victory.

Without doubt, in winning this 1914 Cactus Derby, Oldfield had earned the title "Master Driver of the World."

15

OF TRAGEDIES AND TRIUMPHS

Living close to danger and sudden death produces a fear of the unknown—and racing drivers have always been a superstitious breed. Baby shoes, coins and medals are all part of this ritual—and Oldfield employed a double charm designed to ward off disaster. For years he had worn a "lucky" red-and-white-check Texas bandanna knotted about his throat, but he also carried a folded slip of tattered paper in his coat pocket on which a prayer had been carefully copied by Bess from the original Latin. Barney claimed that the opening words never failed to give him the confidence he needed before a race. They read:

> Whoever shall carry this shall never drown,
> nor meet a death of fury.

(Rickenbacker also kept a copy of the same prayer, and

credited it with saving his life on more than one occasion.)

Since he was involved in so many accidents, Barney was continually worried about false reports of his death being circulated. One such report reached Bess that year, and when Barney reached home he found his wife in tears.

"Don't you ever listen to such crazy talk again," he scolded her. "The only time to believe I'm dead is when I personally walk up and *tell* you so!"

The highly anticipated second running of Corona was set for Thanksgiving Day, 1914, and Oldfield made another sudden team switch for this "circle city" contest, signing to drive for Maxwell at the invitation of team manager Paul Hale Bruske just one day prior to the start.

The 140-hp competition Maxwells, designed by the first "500" winner at Indianapolis, Ray Harroun, were unique in several respects. The flywheel had been eliminated and the crankshaft was counterbalanced, providing an almost vibration-free power plant. Also, oil was pumped out of the engine into a tank, rather than into the crankcase. Harroun's principal innovation consisted of a special carburetor he had tooled to burn kerosene in place of gasoline. To gain the extra heat needed for complete vaporization, the car's exhaust manifold passed through the middle of the engine block, with the exhaust pipe emerging from the left side of the hood directly beneath the carburetor. (When William Carlson drove a Maxwell at Indianapolis that year this marked the first appearance of a kerosene-powered car on the Speedway, earning Carlson his nickname "Coal-oil Billy.")

Burman had blown the engine on his new Peugeot in practice, and Rickenbacker was installed as favorite, having turned the hottest qualifying lap. However, during the race itself, Rick dropped out with assorted mechanical troubles after waging a duel for the lead with Eddie Pullen who went on to win for Mercer. Oldfield's carburetor had been improperly fastened and Barney was unable to challenge Pullen. Nevertheless, he held off such stars as O'Donnell, De Palma and Cooper to finish second over-all despite a stuttering engine and without a single visit to the pits. This constituted a new record, 109 laps nonstop, and won him almost as much acclaim as Pullen's outright victory.

It also demonstrated that Barney could still profit from experience—even after more than two decades of competition. His numerous tire changes at Corona the previous year (before his accident in avoiding the boy) and during the Vanderbilt when De Palma had goaded him into tire-shredding bursts of speed, had earned Barney the reputation of a "rubber-burner," and he had determined to finish nonstop at Corona.

Barney wound up the season with 1,035 points, earned in five national events, to finish third on the 1914 AAA championship list. De Palma had once more gained the crown, and Eddie Pullen had clinched second with his Corona win. This was the closest Oldfield would ever come to the annual AAA title, and a host of crack drivers trailed him in points that year. (Among them: Rickenbacker, Cooper, Mulford, Anderson, Burman, Tetzlaff and O'Donnell.) Most important, however, from Barney's personal standpoint was the fact that he had conclusively proven to his critics that "the old man" was far from a has-been.

In January of 1915 Fred Brooks wrote a lengthy birthday poem honoring Oldfield which was widely reprinted in the press. Stanza upon stanza extolled the virtues of the veteran showman, ending with these words:

> Consider what it means to own
> A name by every mortal known . . .
>
> The free life of the country boy,
> Of meager wants and simple joy,
> Whose sinews grow with outdoor needs,
> His courage by heroic deeds:
> From such as this do great men spring
> As Barney did, the Speedway King,
> Who won the banner fame unfurled—
> "The Master Driver of the World."
>
> We love his grimy, goggled face,
> His matchless daring in a race;
> But greater than his record mile
> Is his great heart and record smile.

Always a sentimentalist, Oldfield was deeply moved by this tribute. It became his most prized item among the many clippings in his burgeoning scrapbooks.

Auto racing threatened to displace baseball as the

national pastime in 1915, and certainly led all other forms of sport across America. A "golden era" of competition on the fast, banked board saucers was underway and before the year had closed, eight major speedways had bowed in, representing a ten million dollar investment. The public road courses were rapidly losing their popular appeal, and high-speed track racing dominated the automotive scene.

For the average motorist, however, long-distance travel by auto was still a bold adventure, and when Hollywood's "Paramount Girl," Anita King, set out on a cross-continental drive from Los Angeles to New York in a Kisselkar her "traveling equipment" included a loaded rifle which she vowed to use on "wild animals and desert bandits." Her daring inspired countless women in America to take up automobiling. What had hitherto been largely the domain of the male was invaded, en masse, by the female, and the auto industry doubled its output over the following year as a result.

For Oldfield, who shared top billing on the Maxwell team with Rickenbacker and Billy Carlson, a series of setbacks marred the opening months of 1915.

In January, at San Diego, his car caught fire on lap 36, and though the flames were extinguished the Maxwell was out. Late February found him at San Francisco for the Grand Prize race, posing for publicity photos with the city's mayor and the governor of California—but again he was a nonfinisher, leaving the contest on lap 29 with a broken piston. (Italian-born newcomer Dario

Resta won for Peugeot, the first of many brilliant successes for the talented young novice.)

On March 6, in the famed Vanderbilt Cup, also held at San Francisco, Barney was never able to bring his Maxwell into serious contention, taking the checker for seventh just ahead of Disbrow's last-place Simplex. (Resta scored his second straight triumph in winning the Vanderbilt.) Carlson's Maxwell took fifth, while Rick did not finish.

Eleven days later, at Venice, Oldfield's luck changed. The Maxwell was now a faster car, since it was decided, after the poor team showing in the Vanderbilt, that the three kerosene-burning machines would be redesigned to run on gasoline. A new exhaust system was therefore fabricated, which allowed the cars to utilize a much more efficient exhaust manifold. As a result, engine power was increased.

In this 300-miler, run on a boards-over-dirt surface, Rickenbacker grabbed the prime slot early in the going, maintaining his lead for 50 blistering laps before retiring with a broken oil line. Dave Lewis, throttling his Stutz up from the pack, took over in the final quarter, with Hearne and Carlson filling out the front runners. Barney was then riding fourth, having narrowly escaped a crash when Jim Parsons' Packard skidded into a banked turn on the backstretch and blew a tire. He missed sideswiping Oldfield by inches.

Close to the finish, Hearne dropped from the fight with oil trouble; then Lewis broke the crankshaft on his Stutz, handing the lead to Carlson with only a single lap remaining. Seeing his chance, Barney leaned hard on the gas and roared by his teammate to win the race in the final dash for the flag.

"I knew that if my cheroot held out I was in the money," quipped the smiling veteran as he gingerly removed the tattered cigar from his mouth. This was another nonstop performance for Oldfield—marking his first major victory in a national championship AAA event.

Barney rapidly followed up Venice with another AAA-sanctioned national win at Tucson, Arizona, over a four-mile desert course on March 20. He was back on the crest of the wave, and not since his Green Dragon days had he experienced such frenzied popular acclaim. Yet he reverted to an old habit which was to cost him a chance to drive that May at Indianapolis: Barney began to spend more time at parties and in bars than he did on the tracks.

On the day of the 500-mile Brickyard classic, set to handle a new French Bugatti which George Hill had brought back from Europe, Oldfield was nursing a head-splitting hangover.

"I couldn't last a lap out there," he told Hill. "The noise alone would kill me! You take over, George."

"All right, Barney, if that's what you want," replied Hill. "I'll do my best."

Hill's best only lasted for 50 short miles. The Bugatti, badly outpaced by much faster machines, was eliminated with a broken pump gear on lap 21. The race went to De Palma, with the amazing newcomer, Dario Resta, in for second.

When Frank Barrieau, the welterweight champion of Canada, defeated Jack Collins of Missouri in a 10-rounder that June, Barney served as referee. Boxing continued to hold great fascination for Oldfield and he attended most of the major fights. At this Barrieau–Collins match he ran into Dave Joyce, an old friend from Chicago. A millionaire, Joyce had made a fortune in lumber, and was noted for his generosity. He had once presented Barney with a $1,000 shotgun as an anniversary gift—and the two men shared a passion for spending money in sizable chunks.

"I hear your contract with Maxwell expired," said Joyce.

"Yeah," sighed Barney. "I got this here Bugatti that Hill brought back, but it's slow as hell. George drove it at Indy and the boys went by him like he was tied to a brick house. George tried to pick up a Mercedes for me overseas, but you know—with the war on he couldn't swing it."

"The French cars seem to be cleaning up," Joyce observed. "Tell you what, Barney—I'll just *buy* you one of 'em as a birthday present. How about a Delage?"

"But, Dave, my birthday was five months ago!"

"So who's counting the days? Do you want a Delage or don't you?"

"Damn right I do!"

"Then you've *got* one."

This 1915 season witnessed the birth of the IMCA (International Motor Contest Association), an organization which was formed to represent the "outlaw" fringe of auto racing. It conducted events at tracks blacklisted by the AAA, and its roster included name drivers currently under AAA suspension or drivers lacking the talent to succeed against seasoned professionals. Barney received an invitation to join the organization and compete as an outlaw at the Nebraska State Fair. The letter hinted that the veteran was too old for anything but hippodroming and warned him that younger stars such as Resta would soon erase his momentary glory. A fat cash guarantee would accompany his acceptance.

Oldfield was furious. He penned a bitterly worded reply in which he declared he would remain loyal to AAA "at any cost." (Actually, with a pair of championship victories to his credit that season, Barney hoped he might yet gain the elusive AAA crown. This undoubtedly influenced his firm decision to stay out of the IMCA.)

While the Delage was being prepared, Barney journeyed to the new plank-track speedway at Tacoma, Washington, on July 2 to unlimber his faithful Christie on the fast, asphalt-coated surface. There he set new half-mile, mile and two-mile records with the aging front-drive, commenting after the runs: "Well, she may be an old girl, but she still has plenty of pep!"

In the Fourth of July feature at Tacoma, for the Montamarathon Trophy, Death rode at the shoulder of jovial, mustachioed Billy Carlson. On lap 60, as the Maxwell ace was booming down the backstretch, one of his tires let go, abruptly catapulting the car over a 30-foot embankment. Neither Carlson nor his mechanic, ex-medical student Paul Franzen, survived the accident.

A shaken Oldfield finished fifth in this tragic contest.

The new Delage proved to be the most unsuccessful car Barney ever drove. Numerous mechanical problems canceled out its speed, and Oldfield never won an important race in the years he was to own the temperamental French machine.

His first outing with the "jinx car" proved a complete fiasco. Barney had issued a challenge to Dario Resta for a match race at the Chicago board speedway in early August, which the Italian promptly accepted. Cooper and Burman joined the lists to make it a four-way meet. Hampered by a malfunctioning carburetor, Oldfield was far behind his three rivals at the end of the 100-mile affair, with Resta's Peugeot easily vanquishing Cooper's Stutz.

At the Elgin Road Races, two weeks later, Barney angrily sailed into the first turn with Anderson and Cooper, at full throttle, stuffing the Delage into a haybale as a result. He eventually finished third behind the two Stutz teammates.

At Fort Snelling, Michigan, in September, with his shock absorbers out of commission, Oldfield had to make 20 pit stops, while Cooper and Anderson finished first and second in a thrilling wheel-to-wheel sprint for the wire.

At Sheepshead Bay a month later, before a "High Society turnout," Barney flogged the Delage to the forefront of the thundering field for seven tours of the newly boarded track. Then he pitted with a broken connecting rod, as Anderson registered a third major win for Stutz. (Another top driver, Harry Grant, met death that season here at Sheepshead Bay in a practice session when his Maxwell crashed and burned.)

Finally, in November, Cooper bested the Oldfield Delage at San Francisco in an Invitational Match (though Barney did manage to outpace Cliff Durant and Tetzlaff).

Therefore, despite his twin victories at Venice and Tucson, Oldfield slipped to seventh position on the 1915 AAA list as Earl Cooper became a two-time champion.

Fred Wagner related an incident which clearly indicated the low morale among members of Oldfield's pit crew during this hard-luck period with the Delage. According to Wagner, Barney had dropped far behind in a California event and was delayed further by several inefficient tire changes.

"What the devil's the matter with you guys?" Barney demanded.

His pit manager shrugged. "We seem to be all out of *esprit de corps*," he replied.

Oldfield frowned, then bellowed: "Then go get some from Harry Stutz. He said I could have anything he had!"

Now desperate to score a win in the Delage, Barney appeared on the grounds of the San Diego Exposition in March of 1916, his jaw set, his mind made up. He would drive the wheels off to finish ahead of the field in this 50-miler!

Burman, Tetzlaff, Durant and Oldfield engaged in a fierce battle from the drop of the flag. Haybales were dislodged as the four men slid wide on turns, each attempting to gain the advantage. On the third lap, diving into a tight curve, Durant, Burman and Tetzlaff all skidded off the course; Barney throttled into the lead with a shout of joy, but his happiness was short-lived. An oil line parted on the Delage, momentarily blinding Oldfield as the thick lubricant sprayed over his goggles. Ripping off his helmet, Barney ducked lower in his seat to escape the spray and continued to drive as Burman took command. When Oldfield rolled under the checker for third he was oil-blackened from head to foot—but at least he had finished the race.

Wild Bob's victory here at San Diego was to be the last in a great career which had seen him rise to the zenith of his dangerous profession, for at Corona, two weeks later, the hard-driving veteran met his end at speed.

His wife had pleaded with Bob not to compete at the big paved circle. She had a vivid dream in which she witnessed her husband's death as a blowout sent his car out of control—and this is precisely what occurred on lap 96 of the main event. Oldfield's Delage had dropped out with engine trouble and Bob was riding second behind Eddie O'Donnell, trying to make up time lost in pit stops, characteristically pushing his light blue Peugeot to its absolute limit, when a left rear tire exploded with the impact of a rifle shot. At 98 mph, Burman couldn't hold the Peugeot on the track; it snapped two heavy posts embedded in concrete, ripped up 100 feet of grass at the edge of the course, struck another car, shearing off the top of the parked vehicle, slammed into the crowd (killing policeman William H. Speers and injuring several spectators), and came to its final rest, 167 yards from the point at which the tire had blown, a smoking mass of wreckage.

Burman died of a fractured skull at Corona's Riverside Hospital while his wife sobbed outside in the corridor. His riding mechanic, Eric Schroeder, also lost his life in the accident.

It was a loss mourned by the entire world of sport.

"Give it up, Barney," pleaded Bess, as she put aside the gaudy newspaper accounts of the Burman crash. "Why do you stay in the game? You've been racing longer than any man in America, and it's time to get out."

"You didn't talk that way eighteen months ago—before the Derby," said Oldfield.

"I knew your pride was involved then," replied his wife. "You had to prove you could still win—and you *did*. There's nothing left to prove now, Barney. You can quit before—"

"Before I end up like Grant, or Bruce-Brown, or Wishart, or Carlson, or Burman. Is that what you're afraid of?"

"Of *course* that's what I'm afraid of. It's what every driver's wife is afraid of, but she doesn't say so because she married her man with her eyes wide open. But now I've got a right to say something. I've watched you risk your life almost every week for a dozen years and I've watched good men die around you, men like Bob Burman, and I've earned the right to ask you to stop. *Will* you stop, Barney?"

"I'll tell you the plain truth, Bess," said Oldfield, "I *was* planning to pull out for good this season, but now I can't. Not since I talked to Harry Miller."

"About what?"

"About a new car, a special job that won't be like anything else on the tracks. It'll be crash-proof, for one thing. Shaped like a torpedo with the driver's seat enclosed. If you roll over, your head is protected. Bob might be alive today if he'd been in a car like the one Miller's gonna build for me."

"Then you won't change your mind? You won't retire?"

"Not yet, not till I see how this new baby goes. Another season—maybe two, then I'm out. And that's a promise."

"I've had my say," Bess told him. "You know my feelings and I know yours. For now, we'll leave things that way."

The Oldfield–De Palma feud flared up again that year at Indianapolis. The rules specified that all entries must be filed by May 1, and De Palma's arrived two days beyond the deadline. It was then necessary for all legally entered drivers to okay De Palma's entry in order for him to compete. Barney refused, pointing out that the rules should stand as written. ("I oughta know. Every time I've broken one somebody steps on my neck!") This left Ralph out of the 1916 classic, and heightened the basic antagonism between the two speed idols. As an example of this, De Palma refused to allow Firestone tires to be used on any car he drove simply because they were publicly endorsed by Oldfield.

The most exciting news of the meet had to do with Barney's famous killer Christie, now ancient by racing-car standards. On May 28, the "master driver" trundled the front-drive machine out to the Brickyard for a shot at the official track record then held by Georges Boillot (who had circled the big Speedway in 1914 at 99.7 miles per hour).

On the previous afternoon's run the gasoline tank had vibrated loose on the uneven brick surface as Oldfield accelerated out of a turn, and he had been forced to reach back and hold the tank steady with one hand, steering with the other. Obviously the tired machine was too old to sustain such all-out efforts, and any number of vital parts might give way in this attempt to surpass Boillot's time.

Carl Fisher was concerned for Oldfield's safety. "Barney, if you'll sell me the Christie right now, I'll take that damned pile of junk into the infield and burn it. It's a death-trap on wheels!"

Oldfield grinned. "I got a hunch she's still the fastest sprinter in the country. Tell you what I'll do, Carl. I been admirin' that white Stetson of yours. If you'll bet it against my busting the record I'll promise to buy you five more like it if I don't break 100 out there today. If I *do* break 100, the hat's mine."

"You'll probably break your *neck* instead," said Fisher, "but it's a deal."

The ugly-snouted red car was warmed up, and Oldfield slid into the driving seat. Barney moved out slowly onto the 2.5-mile track, then began picking up speed as he gradually opened the throttle. The Christie's nose wavered slightly as Oldfield leaned on the gas. He circled faster, passing the main stands where the packed spectators craned their necks to see him hammer by. Oldfield was now ready to go for the record—and he gave a thumbs-up signal to the timer.

The next lap would tell the story.

Hugging the bricks, the red car shot by the timing stand, a bullet fired from a giant gun, and the seconds began ticking away on the official watches. Oldfield rammed into the first turn with the treacherous Christie wide open, sliding to the outside. He corrected, keeping his foot hard down as the tires screamed against the track surface. On the north turn the car appeared to rise up; it seemed to shake and twist itself like a frenzied animal as Barney fought the wheel. Would he die here, on the famed oval, after so many hairbreadth escapes?

No. The Christie straightened, aimed for the tape. With a sulphurous rush it was past—and the lap time was posted for the vast crowd to see: 1:27.7, for an average speed of 102.6 mph. He had done it.

Barney Oldfield became the first driver in history to

lap the Indianapolis Speedway at over 100 miles per hour.

Braking at the pits, Oldfield extended one hand toward Carl Fisher. "My hat, if you please!"

Local papers described that record run as "one of the most spectacular, death-defying drives ever seen anywhere . . ." and Barney later recalled it as "a real hair-raiser." He stated: "I thought when I hit that first turn I'd never come through it alive, but I did. Then, on the next I sure thought my end had arrived, but I made that one too. That car was about ready to fall apart, but somehow we both got around in one piece!"

(Speedway officials decided to shorten the race itself to 300 miles due to the heavy proportion of 500-mile events run over the past months—and Dario Resta easily won with his Peugeot. As in 1914, Oldfield took fifth with the Delage.)

In order to promote interest in the fast Maywood board track in Chicago that June, the management declared that they would pay $2,500 to any driver who could better the 118-mph record set by Jean Chassagne on the Brooklands Speedway in England. To earn the full amount, the driver must also break one minute around the two-mile track.

Oldfield accepted the conditions, and vowed he would win the money with his Christie. But the old chariot was not quite up to this kind of speed. Barney had clocked 113 mph when the cylinders began to freeze, and he limped in with a smoking engine.

"She's done," said Oldfield. "Fisher was right; she's ready for the scrap heap."

The car was sold that same weekend—but this was not the end of the Christie. It was subsequently exhibited by its new owners under a circus tent in many towns across the nation. At ten cents a head, men, women, and children were admitted inside to have a close look at the killer machine which, as the accompanying placard proclaimed, "could only be tamed by the world's Master Driver."

Walter Christie had provided Oldfield with a truly sensational machine, but another unique car was now being readied by engineering genius Harry Miller—a car that would prove to be just as sensational as the immortal front-drive.

The birth of the "Golden Sub" was at hand.

16

THE WEIRD AND WONDERFUL GOLDEN SUB

Harry Armenius Miller was a volcanic forty-one-year-old Los Angeles inventor-engineer with a wizard's touch for motors. It was Miller, in 1914, who had taken the many scattered parts of the complex French-designed Peugeot engine which Bob Burman had blown to bits and painstakingly rebuilt it, actually improving the original in the process. Miller was also the designer behind the famous Master Carburetor (perfected in 1905), and was destined to become one of the most famous figures in the sport over the coming years. (His Miller Specials dominated the Indianapolis Speedway for two decades, and—with Fred Offenhauser and Leo Goossen—he fathered the immortal four-cylinder Offenhauser engine.)

In the fall of 1916 he was hard at work on a special

lightweight four-cylinder engine utilizing aluminum-alloy pistons. It was rated at 130 hp "and should," he informed Oldfield, "produce a top speed of over 120 in the right chassis."

Barney's suggestion for an enclosed-cockpit "crash-proof" machine led to an agreement: Miller would build an Oldfield Special, powered by his new lightweight engine. It would require almost twelve months to complete, and would cost $15,000.

"The car will be ready for the 1917 season," promised Miller, "and it won't look like anything else on the tracks."

The promise was kept.

When the new racer was unveiled at Chicago's Maywood Speedway in June of the following year, just two months after the United States entered World War I, sports reporters in the Windy City were stunned.

With its aluminum top steel-braced and electrically welded, and its streamlined torpedo body painted a glistening metallic gold, the Oldfield Special was indeed impressive. A second bucket seat was provided inside next to the driver for Barney's riding mechanic, Waldo Stein, and Oldfield peered out from an eye-level series of rectangular portholes overlaid with steel netting.

"Glimpsed from a distance, it's a nightmare version of a U-boat," wrote one startled newsman. "Bright yellow, spouting black smoke from its tail, it resembles the fabled golden egg laid by some monstrous goose of prehistoric times!"

Will Pickens, who was again handling Barney's publicity, blandly assured the press that Barney would use a periscope in guiding the car. "That way," said Pickens, "he can see *above* the dust."

Even Oldfield was annoyed at this exaggeration. "Why do you go around tellin' everybody I'm gonna use a periscope, Will?" he asked. "Hell, makes me look like an idiot. I want people to take this car serious."

Pickens chuckled. "How can anybody take a car that looks like an egg on wheels serious? Thing's a freak—and we might just as well milk it for laughs. You know De Palma's gonna run rings around you in that big 12-cylinder Packard of his."

"Like sin he will! Harry says we ought to get 120 easy out of her, maybe more. Anyway, she'll be plenty fast enough to run that spaghetti-eater into the boondocks!"

Pickens immediately informed newsmen that the Oldfield Special was capable of 180 miles per hour, and that Barney would have to undergo an intensive medical examination in order to make certain his body could withstand such blinding speeds.

The old ballyhoo master had lost none of his talent.

On the boards at Maywood, in its qualifying runs, the Golden Sub failed to set any records. It was officially clocked at 107.4—while De Palma ran his Packard Twin-Six around in 110 flat to earn the pole, with Louis Chevrolet's Frontenac edging out Oldfield at 107.8. During the 250-mile race Barney dropped out early in the going with engine "bugs"—causing one reporter to caustically refer to the new special as "The Golden Lemon."

Oldfield was quick to defend his Miller-engined creation. "She'll soon be ready to show what she can do," he said, "and I'll meet De Palma on the dirt at the State Fair in Milwaukee on the twenty-fifth. That is, if he's got enough nerve to show up!"

A nettled De Palma quickly accepted the challenge. "Tell that moon-faced cigar-chewer to stay out of my way," he warned. "I haven't forgotten that blackball he gave me at Indianapolis!"

Thus, in the best tradition of the dime thriller, auto racing's bitterest rivals were once more to clash at speed.

The first round went to Oldfield.

Barney was in his element on the mile dirt oval in Milwaukee, and the Golden Sub performed beautifully, running away from De Palma's big Packard in three straight heat races.

However, on July 29, in Atlanta, with Barney pressing a scant half-car length behind the Twin-Six, the Sub's right front wheel parted from the chassis. For a full 75 yards the Sub skidded along the dirt, its naked axle plowing up billows of dust. Car and driver were about to plunge through the outside fence into a lake when the wild ride ended.

Oldfield stepped out, wiping his brow with his lucky bandanna. "This is one match," he grinned, "that I freely concede to Ralph."

On the boards at Sheepshead Bay, in August, the Packard outran the Sub in a dazzling display of speed before a record crowd. (Even in defeat, Barney received $7,500 from a total gate receipt of $75,000.)

Stubbornly, Oldfield fought back—and at Providence the two rivals staged a vicious battle for the match. Barney had taken the first heat, De Palma the second. Of the final heat, Ralph later wrote: "In this third run, which would decide the over-all winner, I was determined to hold Barney off, and I had picked up a slight lead. Oldfield always caught me on the turns, though I had more speed on the straights. On the last lap I had what I considered a safe lead. I pulled down on the inside of the banking on the final turn, leaving only a thin slit of space between my Packard and the rail. Since Barney was behind me on the upper part of the banking I counted myself a sure winner. Imagine my surprise when Oldfield swooped down across the track, lightning fast, and shot by me, hugging the rail, to take a five-yard lead. I hit the gas, but Oldfield beat me to the flag by the width of a tire. Barney had to come down that bank at full speed, then straighten up his car to slip by. It was a stunt requiring immense strength, keen eyesight—and foolhardy nerve; a stunt I wouldn't dream of trying. A variation of six inches would have meant almost certain death —yet to beat me Barney took a million to one chance and made it."

Although De Palma won again at Detroit, the Sub defeated the Packard at Indianapolis and St. Louis—giving Oldfield the edge that season, four matches out of seven. These bitterly contested duels had attracted hordes of spectators, and both men garnered solid profits. When one newspaper accused the pair of "jockeying" the events Barney heatedly denied the charge.

"I will say that De Palma would never on earth let me beat him if he could help it—and if Ralph licked me it was because there was no way on earth *I* could help it."

Between matches, Oldfield took the Sub to the Maxwelton mile track in St. Louis "to prove that the car was no lemon."

Barney did just that. Letting the Sub have full throttle, he established the Miller machine as the fastest dirt-tracker in the world.

"I had sent to AAA headquarters for the electrical timing machine and a man to operate it," related Barney. "I began by breaking Louis Disbrow's mile record, taking it from 46⅗ seconds to an even 45. Then I made five miles in 3:53.6, as against 4:06.6. The ten-mile record I put at 7:56.2, to offset the old mark of 8:16.4. Then it was twenty miles in 15:52.2 instead of 16:25.6; twenty-five miles in 19:57.6 instead of 20:28.8. Finally, my fifty-mile record was 40:47.6 as against the old one of 40:57.8."

After more than a decade Oldfield had again matched his Green Dragon supremacy—and by season's end he held all dirt-track records from one to 100 miles in Harry Miller's weird and wonderful Golden Sub.

At Springfield, the year almost ended in disaster. On the fairgrounds track, at the far end of the first turn, the car got away from Oldfield, skidding for the outside fence. Barney overcorrected, and the Sub whipped across the course, smashed through the inside fence and turned over. Thrown abruptly forward against the dash, Barney was stunned. A jagged two-by-four from the splintered fence had knifed through the aluminum skin of the top, passing between Oldfield's back and the seat. Gasoline began spraying up from a ruptured fuel line, soaking Barney's trousers—and he heard the dry crackle of flame as the car began to burn.

"Hey—somebody! Get me outa here!" he yelled, pushing desperately against the single door, now jammed tight as a result of the crash. In another moment the back of his shirt was afire—and still the door would not budge.

The image of Harry Grant dying in flames at Sheepshead Bay must surely have been in Oldfield's mind as he made a final wrenching effort to force the door. It popped open, and he lunged for safety, tangling his left foot in the wreckage as he did so. By the time he could shake himself free the hair was aflame on his head. Gasping, half-choked by the billows of smoke, he staggered toward the infield just as the gas tank exploded, spilling him face-forward into the dust.

Among the many spectacular smashups in his daredevil career this was perhaps his closest brush with death. Barney's "crash-proof" automobile had almost become his coffin.

When Bess rushed to his bedside at the hospital she found him conversing loudly with a nurse.

"Oh, Bess, girl—I'm sure glad you got here," he said,

agony in his tone. "Somethin' terrible has happened!"

His wife went pale, expecting news of serious internal injuries. "What, Barney—*what?*"

"They're tryin' to kill me," he said, scowling at the stern-visaged nurse. "They just *won't* lemme smoke cigars in bed!"

When the United States became involved in the European conflict Eddie Rickenbacker had just returned from overseas, where he had been in negotiation to obtain an English Sunbeam racing car. Back in New York, in a special press interview, he cited the splendid records of European competition drivers who were now fighting in the air with the same zest and skill they had employed on the tracks. (Georges Boillot, the Indianapolis lap holder prior to Oldfield's effort with the Christie, had been shot from the skies, but he had been holding off five German planes when he was downed.)

"Racing drivers make natural fliers," Eddie stated. "They have nerve; they understand the concept of speed; they can judge distances—and they possess sound mechanical knowledge. I therefore propose that we form a squadron made up of U. S. racing drivers. In my opinion, we'd be invincible."

De Palma, Pete Henderson, Billy Chandler, Eddie Pullen and Lou Disbrow all volunteered to accompany Rickenbacker into the skies, and he contacted the War Department with his plans. They were not impressed, and shelved the idea. (When the United States entered the war the country was in no valid position to consider

Rickenbacker's plan—since only 55 planes were found to be capable of flight, and these were generally outdated training craft. Mass production, over the following 19 months, resulted in a total of 12,000 planes, but the opening months of the conflict were grave ones.)

Rick later received a phone call from Washington. Did he wish to report immediately for overseas service as a driver in General Pershing's motor corps? He must accept at once. Eddie said yes—knowing that once he had reached France he would be able to effect a transfer to the aviation corps. (This was accomplished with the aid of Billy Mitchell—and Rick personally accounted for 26 enemy planes in five months of air action, becoming one of America's greatest air aces.)

Oldfield had also sent in his application as a potential aviator, but he was turned down for active duty because he was overage. Barney was then forty, and had no choice but to cancel his plans to enter the service.

He went to work rebuilding the Sub, stripping the car of its confining metal top—and appeared on the line in mid-January of 1918 at Ascot Speedway to challenge Louis Chevrolet's six-cylinder Frontenac. Barney took the match by winning the first and third heats with the stripped machine, satisfying himself that the Springfield crash had not affected the Sub's blistering speed.

The sensation of this match at Ascot was a stunt flying exhibition by nineteen-year-old Katherine Stinson, a Pickens discovery who was called "the female Beachey."

The girl had come to the attention of Will Pickens in

1913, when she asked him for a job with his Flying Circus. (Will was promoting dozens of high-flying daredevils during this period.) After she proved her ability, he agreed to manage the tiny Southern aviatrix, billing her as "The Schoolgirl Who Outflies the Men," and in two years she had become one of his biggest attractions. It was Katherine Stinson who originated sky-writing at night when she wrote C A L (for California) in the sky above Los Angeles in 1915, tracing the letters with magnesium flares tied to the wings of her Wright. She also was the first woman to loop in a plane of her own design, using the Gnome rotary motor from Beachey's ill-fated Taube. During the later stages of the war she trained hundreds of fliers for the Allied armies at the Stinson Flying School in San Antonio, and her brother Eddie Stinson, who was one of her pupils, also went on to great fame as a flier and plane designer.

Barney set a new mile record in mid-March in qualifying the Sub for the "Blinkey Ben" Trophy event at the Ascot Speedway, but was beaten in the contest itself by upcoming Tommy Milton. Kept out of service by the fact that he was blind in his right eye, this future road ace was just beginning to rate the attention of the experts. His career was actually being launched as Oldfield's was ending.

After the race Milton approached Barney's pit.

"I'd like to ask a favor," he said.

"You sure musta wanted that 'Blinkey Ben' trophy

damn bad," growled Oldfield. "You knew I was after it, didn't ya?"

Milton nodded.

"Then what the devil are you doing here in my pit askin' favors?" demanded Barney.

"Well . . . I need tires for the main event," Milton said softly. "I thought maybe you'd let me borrow some of yours."

"Well, what a colossal nerve!" marveled Oldfield. "Beats me blue, then comes to ask for my tires."

Milton flushed, and turned to leave.

"Wait a minute!" snapped Barney. He gestured to his mechanic. "Waldo, give this nervy bastard anything he needs."

Milton mumbled his thanks, but Oldfield continued to scowl.

"You sure musta wanted that 'Blinkey Ben' trophy damn bad," he repeated slowly.

Milton grinned—and the two men were friends from that day forward.

The AAA, late the previous year, had offered to call a halt to all sanctioned meets, but President Wilson informed the governing organization that such a step was not necessary. Therefore, in May of 1918, with the war still raging in Europe, a crowd of 18,000 gathered to witness the first official championship race of the season at Uniontown, Pennsylvania. Before the event got underway a track official announced that the U. S. wanted auto racing to continue "to aid in the testing and development of motors."

Barney was again runner-up in a heat race here at Uniontown losing first place to Ralph Mulford, and it was apparent that the Sub was not being pressed to its limit. A third, a fifth and sixth in other events over the following two months substantiated the fact that Oldfield was finally slowing down. In September, via a terse message from Washington, the fuel administration requested that all automotive competition cease—and the AAA immediately met the request.

"I'd quit too," Oldfield told pressmen, "but I've got a contract to fulfill."

Barney had signed for a brief farewell junket (under the supervision of J. Alex Sloan) and when he appeared at the Michigan State Fair that same month the AAA again branded him an "outlaw," placing him under permanent suspension.

"That's all right by me," Barney told reporters. "I'm signed for one more match in Missouri. Then I'll be glad to hang up the goggles for good."

Oldfield kept his word. On October 13, at Independence, he rolled the battle-scarred Golden Sub into action for the last time, defeating local favorite Ray Lamkin's Duesenberg in two straight heats around the half-mile dirt oval.

After 25 years of speed on bike paths, horse tracks, open roads and paved speedways the king of auto racing had stepped down from his throne.

By the close of 1918, AAA records placed Barney

eighth in the list of surviving point holders, compiled from contests run over the years 1909-1918. Oldfield had driven in 36 championship events to garner a total of 3,180 points. (Barney later estimated that he had competed in some 2,000 events in all, beginning in 1902 with Ford's 999.) De Palma headed the list, having earned 10,300 points in the 62 championship races he'd driven. The others, rated above Oldfield for this 10-year period, were Cooper, Resta, Mulford, Rickenbacker, Anderson and Pullen.

In placing Barney in his true perspective it must be noted that he was at his competitive peak on the dirt horse tracks during his Green Dragon days, and that only Oldfield among the many star drivers of that earlier era had remained active in the sport, having made the difficult transition from dirt oval to road to speedway. Yet this durable performance did not explain his undisputed pre-eminence.

Drivers such as Burman, De Palma and Cooper amassed a much greater number of victories, and were without question Barney's superiors in over-all driving skill, yet they never matched his incredible public appeal. Barney was "of the people," and the public identified with him as they identified with no other driver of his time. From his gaudy ties to his barroom brawls he was a "regular guy." Burman was as daring; Cooper was as stubborn; De Palma was as publicity-conscious; Tetzlaff was as aggressive and hard-living, yet no other driver combined *all* these colorful traits. When he stood up in the back of a racing car and shouted out his famous greeting: "You know me, Barney Oldfield!" the public responded with an open heart. Win or lose, he was their true speed idol, and no one else, and when he raced it was as though they watched themselves out on the track at speed—and up to the point of his retirement no other active sports champion had ever occupied the throne of popularity for such an incredible span of years.

Fred Wagner paid the veteran a heartfelt farewell tribute when the beloved starter broke a long-standing rule (never to place any one of his "boys" above another) and publicly acclaimed Barney as the most famous figure the sport had ever produced.

"He has made his name a synonym for auto racing, through achievements that need no word of praise from me, and by a sense of showmanship worthy of Barnum and Belasco. In fact," added Wagner, "when the final trumpet sounds and I am speeding to reach the pearly gates before they swing closed I should not be in the least surprised to have a celestial traffic cop stop me and growl: 'Say, who do you think you are, Barney Oldfield?' "

of t
sip]
cha
gue
wei
Wi
  S
We
  ]
he

  ]
its
on
A]
the
ye
ru
tir

a
ni
na

li
fo
p;
ai
st
se

17

LIFE WITH FIRESTONE

In November of 1918 the war ended. That "dirty job" in Europe had been attended to; the Kaiser had fled into Holland, and Johnny came marching home. Thus the door was opened on a new competitive season in 1919. Responding to public demand that Oldfield be allowed to compete again in sanctioned meets, AAA's chairman Kennerdell lifted Barney's suspension, providing the sum of $1,000 was forthcoming.

The fine was never paid. Oldfield had no intention of returning to the tracks; thanks to Harvey Firestone, Barney was now a full-fledged tire tycoon and his Golden Sub was in the hands of mechanic-driver Waldo Stein.

Actually, this business enterprise was the brainchild of Henry Ford, who personally brought the idea to Firestone.

"Look, Harvey," Ford had said to him, "I know you've

211

down the back stairs to end up on Howard Street in a "blind pig," sipping bootleg whiskey and exchanging wisecracks and sports gossip with the denizens of the famed saloon district.

And invariably on a Saturday night—since prohibition was in full flower—Barney would be hauled down to the local station house with ex-prizefighters in a sirening "paddy wagon," where a bond would be issued for the business tycoon's immediate release. (Harvey Firestone was wise enough to have a man on duty at the police station each Saturday evening whose sole job it was to bail out Oldfield before the press arrived.)

In desperation, fearing a scandal, Firestone moved the offices of the Oldfield Tire Company to Cleveland in order to get Barney away from "unsavory influences," but the pattern remained unchanged. Within a week after his new office had opened in Cleveland, Oldfield was as well-known on notorious Woodward Avenue as he had ever been on Howard Street.

Drawn by the roar of racing engines and his many friends in the sport, Barney attended most of the major events across the country. When the new Beverly Hills Speedway opened in February of 1920 Oldfield was there, sharing a front-row grandstand with such cinema personalities as Doug Fairbanks, Charlie Chaplin, Wallace Beery and Tom Mix, all of whom were racing fans. Cecil B. De Mille was one of the track's founding fathers, and no expense was spared to make the new speedway the Taj Mahal of board tracks.

play
mone
it's go
"Al
real r
be in
office.
"D:
I shou
How
"I'
right
In
filed
a pro
stone
By
Mrs.
gan a

Young Jimmy Murphy (who was destined to win this inaugural event as well as many other important races in his brilliant career) took Chaplin around the big track at speed; then Doug Fairbanks toured the course with De Palma. Watching from the stands, Tom Mix turned to Oldfield.

"Looks easy," he said. "Bet I could take my Stutz Bearcat around almost that fast."

Barney shook his head. "Those turns are banked more than 45 degrees. I'll bet you couldn't even turn a fast lap without spinning."

The wager was accepted, and Oldfield arranged to have Mix take his Stutz onto the track. Tom waved to the crowd, then shot off, tires squealing. On one of the high-banked turns he discovered that fast driving involved more than a heavy throttle foot. Mix lost the big Stutz on the banking, slid backwards along the boards, then looped tail for nose.

Back in the stands the red-faced western star confronted a grinning Oldfield. "Don't feel so bad, Tom," Barney told him. "Hell, I can't ride a nag any better than you can drive that Bearcat!"

That same year Oldfield was invited to Havana along with Joe Boyer, Tommy Milton, Louis Chevrolet, Eddie Hearne, Ira Vail, Roscoe Sarles and Pete De Paolo. Barney was to serve in the capacity of race referee, since the Cuban promoters were aware that his name would bring them some extra publicity. They got more than

18

FROM LOST FORTUNES TO A DREAM AT DAYTONA

Oldfield embarked on his third matrimonial voyage in the midst of the Roaring Twenties, a time of vast optimism on Wall Street and savage gangland violence in Chicago. This was the jazz-filled era of F. Scott Fitzgerald, of bathtub gin and bobbed hair. Flappers danced the Charleston on speakeasy tables while Rudolph Valentino induced palpitations of the heart among countless housewives at neighborhood picture palaces. The world of sports rang to the exploits of Jack Dempsey, Gene Tunney (who read Shakespeare), Red Grange, Bobby Jones, Babe Ruth and Lou Gehrig.

"People are livin' high these days," Oldfield told his new bride, "and I aim to live it up with the best of 'em. For a start, just to prove that old Barney knows how to

218

treat his women, I'm gonna buy you a diamond ring that'll knock your eyes out, an' I aim to shell out eighteen grand for that sparkler. An' that, like they say, is only the beginning!"

Hulda Rae Braden was a thirty-five-year-old widow. She had been married twice in the past before she met Oldfield at San Diego, her home town. When Barney asked Hulda to become his third wife he promised her that they would tour Europe together—and his post-wedding gift was the $18,000 diamond ring.

Prior to this sudden marriage, the veteran had planned to manufacture an automobile, bearing his name, and had driven a prototype to Indianapolis that June. A three-passenger coupe of "rakish design," the car featured an overhead valve engine which delivered 75 horsepower, and was to go into mass production in 1926. Instead, Barney spent several months of the year overseas with his new bride, and final plans for the Oldfield failed to materialize.

May 21, 1927, was an important date for America. On this day Lindbergh landed the *Spirit of St. Louis* in Paris after his heroic solo flight across the Atlantic, and the newspapers of the globe saluted "Lucky Lindy" with headlines and feature stories.

Another record was made on May 21, important only to those in the auto industry—and to Barney Oldfield. The ex-speed king climbed into a Hudson "Super 6" coach and set a new world's thousand-mile nonstop stock car record at Culver City, California, by circling the banked board saucer for 13 hours, 8 minutes, averaging 76.4 mph.

"Does this mean you're going back into competition, Barney?" asked a mechanic as Oldfield wearily rolled the car into the pits.

Barney shook his head. "Nope. I'm a financier from here on out. This run was just one of a kind. Why risk my neck on a track for peanuts when I can risk it on the stock market for millions?"

(Guided by the wise tips of numerous influential "inside" friends, Oldfield's investments had quickly multiplied and his personal fortune in stocks climbed rapidly toward the half-million mark.)

That June, Barney drove the Hudson to New York where he led a parade of classic cars down Broadway. On a float directly behind him, in the place of honor, was old 999. The machine had been rescued from oblivion by Henry Ford, and was now once again the property of the renowned industrialist.

Oldfield enjoyed the limelight and the cheering crowds, and he never overlooked a chance to keep his name before the public. His appearance still drew wild applause whenever he turned up at a major sport event— and four lines from a poem by William Herschell sum up the affection his name engendered:

> "Yes, Barney's here!" they cried,
> "The starting bomb can shoot!
> 'Twould be no race at all without
> Oldfield and his cheroot!"

In this get-rich-quick period, when the Wall Street ticker tapes sang their golden song, the skies seemed to be raining money. The National Association of Merchant Tailors declared that a properly dressed American should own twenty suits, a dozen hats, eight overcoats and twenty-four pairs of shoes. Advertisements for $50,000 Russian sables vied with $45,000 duplex apartments on the same page. A New York jeweler casually offered a pearl necklace for $685,000, and John Raskob, vice-president of General Motors, wrote a widely quoted article for the *Ladies Home Journal.* Its title: "Everybody Ought to Be Rich."

Certainly Barney Oldfield agreed with this idea as his investments continued to build.

"On October 1, 1929, my account in Detroit stood at just over one million dollars," he later recalled. "I had 22,500 shares on margin, and my annual income was $270,000. Before the year was over I didn't have a cent!"

Oldfield's paper fortune literally disappeared overnight when the stock market crashed during "Black October" of '29. (No clearer word-picture has been drawn of the terrible chaos on the floor of the Stock Exchange than that provided by a guard who was present at the scene: "They roared like a lot of lions and tigers. They hollered and screamed, they clawed at one another's collars. It was like a bunch of crazy men. Every once in a while, when Radio or Steel or Auburn would take another tumble, you'd see some poor devil collapse and fall to the floor.")

Barney refused to panic. Money had always slipped

from his grasp during his profitable career, and this was simply a more crippling variation on a familiar theme.

He turned to his public, becoming a ballyhoo man for thrill shows, and often served in an official capacity at speed meets in various cities.

It was during this period that ex-driver Ira Vail asked Oldfield to act as honorary starter for the Syracuse 100-miler at the New York State Fair.

Upon his arrival Barney was met by Vail and taken directly to the local newspaper office for an interview.

"We need a little pre-race publicity," said the sports editor. "You know what I'm after—a statement with some *bite* to it."

"Well—" began Oldfield, "you can say how happy I am to be here in your wonderful city and how proud I am to be chosen to start this great race."

The editor looked disappointed; obviously he had been hoping for something more original. He tried again. "I'd like your opinion, as an expert, on our present-day drivers, the boys you'll be flagging off at Syracuse tomorrow. But first, to satisfy my own curiosity, let me ask you a few personal questions."

"Shoot," said Barney.

As the editor fired one question after another at Oldfield, all of them dealing with the veteran's stormy relationship with the AAA, Oldfield's temper began to assert itself. His replies became heated—and soon Barney was loudly denouncing the entire organization.

"Hold on there," the editor interrupted. "Most of our current drivers get along just *fine* with the AAA."

Red with rage, Barney waved his cigar in the air like a sword. "Yeah, an' I'll tellya what kind of drivers you got runnin' for you—bums! That's all they are, bums! There's not a single one of 'em could last a lap in my day!"

The editor had found his statement—and Ira Vail had lost a starter. When the field for Syracuse was flagged away that weekend Barney was headed back to California.

Henry Ford's financial empire had survived the crash of '29, and his power and influence as a major American industrialist remained in full force during the bleak depression days of the thirties. Ford's friendship with Oldfield had never lessened over the years, and when Hank met Barney at Indianapolis reporters were on hand for the occasion. The two pioneers shook hands warmly as Hank declared: "We started together at the bottom and we owe each other a lot. After all, it could be said that you made me and I made you."

Oldfield grinned, flipping open an empty wallet. "Yeah—but I did a damn sight better job of it than you did!"

In 1931 Oldfield joined Hudson Motors as a road tester. He was hired to subject stock cars to rigorous highway trials. That May he drove a Hudson to Indianapolis, serving as official starter for the 500—and proudly announced: "We've become a real family now. Hulda and I have legally adopted a girl, Elizabeth, and we in-

INTO LEGEND

Embittered by his failure to win the backing he needed for his Daytona record attempt, Barney allowed the Los Angeles *Examiner* to use his name as ammunition in an organized battle to close California's Ascot Speedway. In an article headlined: "Auto Races Brutal Says Barney Oldfield," the veteran was quoted: "Automobile racing has outlived its usefulness. It has ceased to be a sport and has become a morbid and brutal spectacle."

Although Ascot's fatality list *was* impressive, this all-inclusive attack on the sport shocked the racing world. This was unfortunate, since Barney never really lost his genuine affection for automotive competition. His words had been delivered in bitterness, and he often expressed regret over their hasty publication. Nevertheless, some of his friends could never forgive him for this public blast at the sport which had made his name famous.

One fact was clear: Barney *was* becoming increasingly safety-conscious as he progressed in years, and when he joined Plymouth as a "highway adviser" he toured several states, lecturing extensively to school and civic groups on the values of safe driving.

"Sixty miles an hour is fast enough for anybody," he told these groups. "When I'm on the road I *never* exceed that figure."

This was a slight exaggeration. On more than one occasion Oldfield found it difficult to follow his own advice. Then his natural competitive spirit would overwhelm him and he would plant his foot on the floorboards in order to experience the familiar sensation of "holding her wide open." He once sideswiped a road grader, overturning his car and breaking his wife's jaw. On another of these nostalgic excursions into the realms of high speed he was pursued by no less than three motorcycle policemen. Two of them abandoned the chase when the pace grew too fierce, but the third finally brought the flying veteran to bay.

The officer's question was inevitable: "Who do you think you are, Barney Oldfield?"

The red-faced safety expert paid his fine in court the next day.

During the summer months of 1934 Barney kept his name before the public by engaging in a series of tractor exhibitions at Midwestern fairs, and also participated in the "Jinx Derby," as a part of the Chicago Fair, "winning" this contest for Old-Timers in a 1904 Maxwell.

He became very active in civic affairs in Beverly Hills, where his $200,000 home was pointed out as a "showplace with the finest olive trees in Southern California."

His married life, however, was an unhappy one. Hulda and Barney quarreled continually, and Oldfield finally moved his scrapbooks and trophies into one small upstairs room, leaving the rest of their plush Beverly Hills home to the occupancy of his third wife.

In 1937 he resigned from Plymouth to open "The Barney Oldfield Country Club" in Van Nuys. Hank Kawalec, who was bartender-manager for the Club prior to Oldfield's purchase, relates how the deal came about: "Barney had been nosing around the place for maybe two weeks before making up his mind to buy, asking me a million questions. Finally I got fed up and told him I had work to do and to go bug somebody else. He blew his stack, and swore that now he was sure as the devil going to buy the joint just so he could have the pleasure of firing me. Next day he was back with the official papers, and I reached for my coat. He wanted to know where I was going, and I snapped back that I had been wanting to get married for a long time anyway and my girl was waiting for me in San Francisco. Since I was fired this was a perfect time to head north. 'How much did they pay you here?' Barney wanted to know, and I told him a hundred bucks a month. He said if I'd stay on he'd double that. Said he liked my nerve, was tired of 'yesmen' and figured we'd get along. Naturally I said sure. Then he handed me a hundred in cash and told me to take a two-week vacation and get married. So off I went, with his money in my pocket, headed for Frisco. That was the kind of guy he was; if he cottoned to you he couldn't do enough for you."

Remembering the good days at the saloon on Spring Street, the many friends who would stop in to drink beer and listen to his stories, Barney made an all-out effort to recapture the past in a modern-day country club setting. Situated in a lush canyon in the San Fernando Valley, the vast layout featured twin tennis courts, a softball diamond, a half dozen large barbecue pits, a 50-by-100-foot swimming pool, a huge ballroom, spacious clubhouse and fifteen acres of shaded picnic grounds.

Since Barney's new establishment was only eight miles from Hollywood he was able to play host to numerous stars of the cinema, and would often turn the club over to a major studio for the weekend. (One of these affairs, involving MGM, netted him $1,700.)

At the Beverly Hills annual Chamber of Commerce banquet in 1940, Barney had his picture taken beside Jack Benny, Groucho Marx, Robert Taylor and Eddie Cantor. He was a celebrity among celebrities, and his name still retained magic. (Billboards that year featured paintings of Oldfield, with cigar, advising motorists to "Buy Polly Gas, it's great on grades!")

In 1941 Barney was hired by Universal as "a technical expert" for the Vanderbilt Cup sequence in *Back Street*, starring Margaret Sullivan, but his connections with the film world failed to keep the Oldfield Country Club in operation as a new global war began.

"Barney opened up the Fox Hills Café," says Kawalec, who accompanied the veteran in this new venture. "He only kept this place for about seven months, then let it go to open the Live Oaks at Van Nuys and Sherman Way. I owned twenty-five per cent of the Oaks, and we made nothin' but money. Paid off our initial investment within four weeks—but it was kinda rough. Soldiers would come in and nearly wreck the joint. Friday and Saturday nights were always the worst. Barney was well into his sixties then, but he was still as strong as a bull. Had huge arms. I saw him lift the back end of a Chevy clear off the ground on a bet . . . Anyhow, on Fridays and Saturdays Barney used to tell me: 'Kid, when the action starts I'll cut the master switch in the kitchen. As soon as those damn lights go off grab a club and start swinging!' I remember after one scrap, when I threw the switch again, there stood Barney with the shirt ripped right off his back. Just had his cuffs, collar and tie on. We sure earned our dough at the Live Oaks."

Oldfield's free-swinging antics put him back in the news during 1944, when he tangled with famed restaurateur "Prince" Mike Romanoff in a Beverly Hills traffic skirmish. Barney claimed that the Prince had cut across his right of way on a turn. Oldfield stopped, jumped out, hauled Romanoff from the seat of his car and accused him of "lousy driving." After a heated argument, Barney swung on the Prince and several blows were exchanged. Romanoff was knocked to the street and Oldfield's glasses were smashed in the melee.

"I got a black eye out of it," Barney commented, "but the Prince was a mess!"

In May of 1945, as the Second World War ended in Europe, Barney sold his country club, which had been long dormant, and purchased a 200-acre oil lease in Oklahoma.

"Hulda had to sell her diamond ring to help finance this thing," says Kawalec. "Barney took me with him out to Oklahoma to work a couple of wells he'd paid $15,000 apiece for. Place was near Beggs, in a desolate stretch, and we had to haul in our own water. We dug the wells ourselves and it was backbreaking work. Turned out they were nearly dry and we were lucky to get out two barrels a day. We spent months out there and finally junked the whole deal. This finished Barney. He looked like a ghost when he headed home, and most of his money was gone."

Back in California, fresh from another bitter quarrel with Hulda, Barney was driving slowly down Wilshire Boulevard in Los Angeles when a siren pulled him to the curb. A burly motor cop walked up to the window of Oldfield's car, his grim expression masking a secret smile. He had recognized the speed veteran and had decided to pull Barney's leg. He'd stop the great man for going too slow!

He leaned forward and growled: "Say, Pop, you know you're in an *automobile*, not a rocking chair. We can't have all the traffic on Wilshire lined up behind you. Lucky you weren't around in the days of Barney Oldfield. Old Barney would have run *you* right off the road!"

233

The officer paus
reply. Instead, the
seat; his hands sli
was barely audible

After a long sile
moved away—leav
by the curb.

The quarrels wi
drinking heavily. I
to erase the prese
the atom, he lived
"the great days" fi
to ask if they rei
Derby, or the tin
Christie at Indian
the Blitzen. And
Barney would sta
could.

Late in 1945 h
"legal residence"
a divorce. Barney
up their unhappy

"We've been b
field. "It had to e

The aging spee
faced the prospe
and nights.

Then Barney g
Oldfield was ove

Henry Ford was there, and so was Ed Apperson, Ransom E. Olds, J. Frank Duryea and Charles King (the first man to drive a motor car in the city of Detroit). These were the trail blazers, the men who had brought the motor car to the average American citizen, and this was their splendid hour.

To thunderous applause, Barney Oldfield proudly accepted the "trophy of progress," honoring him as one of the nation's automotive pioneers. Standing there in Detroit, tears rolling down his cheeks, listening to the applause, he knew that his name had not been forgotten.

It was the finest moment of a fabulous life.

Four months later, while making plans for a fishing trip to Big Bear Lake, Oldfield complained of a severe headache.

"Dunno what it could be," he told Bess. "I've had a couple of these things lately. If they keep up I'll see a doctor when we get back."

Barney never reached Big Bear. On the morning of October 4, 1946, a cerebral hemorrhage abruptly ended his plans. Bess found him when she returned to their room with the morning paper. He appeared to be asleep, but his heart was not beating. After countless crashes on and off the tracks during his violent, hazardous career of speed Barney died peacefully in his bed at sixty-eight.

His death brought a close to an era of giants.

In 1953 he was elected to Auto Racing's Hall of Fame; the beloved, lusty, self-confident daredevil crouched behind a massive wood-rimmed racing wheel with a stubby cigar clamped tight in one corner of his mouth and a competitive gleam in his dark eyes was now immortal.

Berna Eli Oldfield had passed into legend.

BIBLIOGRAPHICAL N

Originally, when this proje
to include a detailed Oldfield bibliograp
research, however, I realized that this v
been dealing with almost any other well
colorful period in history a formal bibli
quite easily. For example, more than a
lished dealing with the life and career of
wished to delve into the lives of Babe
Dempsey, the reader would find that a
amined between hard covers in a variet

Not so with Oldfield.

In 1919 an obscure publishing house
titled: *Barney Oldfield's Book for the N*
sketch by Homer C. George was include
piece represents the only hard-cover tr
was never reprinted.

In 1925 the *Saturday Evening Post* ra
article, "Wide Open All the Way," in
the byline with Oldfield. Unfortunately,
several counts. Sturm obviously took C
faulty memory) for matters which should
Since this *Saturday Evening Post* article

half-dozen major magazine articles on Oldfield (printed since 1925) they contain some of the same errors.

Only two historians, Russ Catlin and J. L. Beardsley, have probed beyond this point with individually researched pieces dealing with Oldfield. Their findings were printed in the now-defunct *Speed Age*— and Catlin's "History of AAA Championship Racing," in nine parts, was outstanding, and well deserves book publication.

Taking these factors into account, I decided against attempting a formal bibliography. Instead, I have chosen to list ten books culled from the many volumes consulted in the preparation of the Oldfield saga. They offer the reader much that is interesting and informative on the pioneer days of racing, and I am happy to recommend them.

Anderson, Rudolph E., *The Story of the American Automobile*, Washington, D.C., Public Affairs Press, 1950.

Bentley, John, *Great American Automobiles*, Englewood Cliffs, N. J., Prentice-Hall, 1957.

Clymer, Floyd (editor and publisher), *Indianapolis Race History*, Los Angeles, Clymer, 1946.

Horsley, Fred, *World's Fastest Cars*, Los Angeles, Trend Inc., 1955.

Lozier, Herbert, *Auto Racing, Old and New*, New York, Fawcett Publications, 1953.

Musselman, M. M., *Get A Horse!*, New York, J. B. Lippincott Company, 1950.

Markmann, Charles L., and Sherwin, Mark, *The Book of Sports Cars*, New York, G. P. Putnam's Sons, 1959.

Nevins, Allan, *Ford: The Times, The Man, The Company*, New York, Charles Scribner's Sons, 1954.

Purdy, Ken W., *The Kings of the Road*, Boston, Atlantic-Little, Brown & Company, 1952.

Wagner, Fred J., *The Saga of the Roaring Road*, Los Angeles, Clymer, 1949.

ACKNOWLEDGMENTS

Writing is supposed to be one of man's lone-
liest professions, and it *is* true that the full-time author
must endure many hours of solitude at the typewriter in
order to transfer his mental images to paper. But when he
steps away from his machine he finds a friendly, recep-
tive world awaiting him. Everyone seems genuinely interested in what he is trying to accomplish, and if help is
requested it is immediately forthcoming. Certainly this
has been my experience in assembling data for *Barney
Oldfield.*

I traveled through several states to gather up the missing threads of Oldfield's life, and in every city I visited
the response to my search was rewarding and heartening.
Time, material, photos and memories were freely shared
and, in each instance, I was freshly spurred on to finish
the project. It is quite doubtful that this book would

INDEX

245